*Coat-of-arms as borne by Zdeněk Brtnický z Valdštejna*
*(Drawn by Jiří Louda)*

ita formatum ut omnibus ex partibus spectatores commodissima singula videre possint. In reditu transivimus pontem magnificis aedificijs ornatum, à quibus uni adhuc affixa cernuntur capita quorundam comitum et nobilium, qui laesae Majestatis rei supplicio affecti sunt.

Die ☿. 4. July.

Deambulatum exivimus, fuimus in templo S. Pauli de quo postea.

Die ♃. 5. July.

Tametsi vedi Westmonasterij urbeculam, plus mill. pass. urbe distantem, sed tamen per suburbia continuatam venimus; sic dictam quod ad occiduam urbis partem sita, templo, foro juridico situ, et Regia celeberrimam. Templum imprimis totius Angliae magnificentissimum et perexcelsum, Regum Angliae inauguratione et sepultura insigne.

*A page from the Diary, actual size, with entries for 4 and 5 July 1600, when Waldstein visited St Paul's Cathedral and Westminster. (Reproduced by kind permission of the Vatican Library)*

Squallet scena, silent scoenæ, nec Musica garrit
Delicium ut nostrum Morlig intemt:
Sed non interijsti, oculis, ore, auribus hæres
Nosq́ erimus lineæ: musica, scena tibi.
Plaudite cui talis transacta est fabula vitæ
Posteritas semper qua facit ee novam.
Wilhelmus Alabaster deflevit,
Obijt anno Domini 1596. 18. April:
Supra pulpitum et Biblia hæc notata invenias:
Beaumonty ipses dedit, atq́ volumina sacra
Duntaxat voluit vetuitq́ papistica ferre.
Æmulationem mutuam exercent hoc et S. Joannis collegium propter pratum quoddam: Regina tamen pro collegio Trinitatis pronunciavit.
Post vidimus Collegium S. Joannis, cuius præfectus olim fuit clarissimus et summæ eruditionis Theologus Witakerus; cui etiam in sacello positum est monumentum, cum hac inscriptione.
Hic situs est Doctor WITAKERUS regius olim
Scripturæ interpres, quem ornabat gratia Linguæ
Judiciiq́ acies, et lucidus ordo memorq́,
Lectus, et invictus labor et sanctissima vita
Næ sed enituit virtus rarissima, fatos

*Collegium Joannis*

Valdštejna, Zdeněk Brtnický z, baron, 1581-1623.

# THE DIARY OF BARON WALDSTEIN

*A Traveller in Elizabethan England*

TRANSLATED AND ANNOTATED

BY G. W. GROOS

With 48 illustrations,
4 in colour

THAMES AND HUDSON

Any copy of this book issued by the publisher as a paperback is sold subject to the condition that it shall not by way of trade or otherwise be lent, re-sold, hired out or otherwise circulated, without the publisher's consent, in any form of binding or cover other than that in which it is published and without a similar condition including these words being imposed on a subsequent purchaser.

© 1981 Thames and Hudson Ltd, London
First published in the USA in 1981 by Thames and Hudson Inc., 500 Fifth Avenue, New York, New York 10110

Library of Congress Catalog Card Number 81-50795

All rights reserved. No part of this publication may be reproduced or transmitted in any form or by any means, electronic or mechanical, including photocopy, recording, or any information storage and retrieval system, without permission in writing from the publisher.

Text and monochrome illustrations printed in Great Britain
by BAS Printers Ltd, Over Wallop, Hampshire
Colour illustrations printed in Great Britain
by Balding + Mansell Ltd, Wisbech, Cambridgeshire
Bound in Great Britain by The Pitman Press, Bath

# CONTENTS

Foreword     7

Introduction

     *The Diary and the Diarist*     10

     *Other Diarists*     17

     *The Mechanics of the Translation*     18

     *The Notes*     20

     *Bibliography*     20

Map showing the route of Waldstein's tour     22

THE DIARY AND NOTES     24

Nota Bene     182

Index     182

وقل رب زدني علماً

Upon the recommendation of a committee of the Faculty of Arts,
King Abdulaziz University
in the
Kingdom of Saudi Arabia
gave a subsidy covering a substantial part of the production costs
of this volume in order to encourage research and promote
the publication of works of scholarly interest.
Thames and Hudson and the translator
of Waldstein's Diary wish to thank the University
for this most generous gift.

I wish to record my most grateful thanks to the Holy See
for permission to translate and publish part
of Waldstein's Diary; also to the Father Prefetto
of the Vatican Library for his great kindness
in allowing me – since it was my only opportunity
of being in Rome that year – to make
use of the Library at a time when it was officially
closed for the vacation.

G.W.G.

# FOREWORD

Translators are compulsive writers of forewords, and they are scarcely to be blamed. They feel acutely vulnerable: every page which they have written has made them liable to be accused of equal and opposite errors: errors of pedantic slavishness to the original *and* of unjustified freedom of expression; of undue modernisms of language and also of forsoothly and thusly affectation. The preface is the translator's one opportunity of self-defence, and invariably he seizes it. Look only at the best-known translators of Homer and you will find that Chapman* does it, that Pope does it, that Samuel Butler does it, and that Robert Graves does it also. They were of course quite wrong to imagine that it would do them any good: fourteen pages of self-justification did not in the least shield Francis Newman (brother of the Cardinal) from Matthew Arnold's sarcasms; Messrs Butcher and Lang tell us how right they were to imitate the noble 'somewhat antiquated prose' of the Authorized Version for their rendering, and W. H. D. Rouse (in *his* preface) explains just why they were wrong, giving the reasons which ought to compel us to prefer his own clever and somewhat self-consciously modern style.

As for my own translation, I shall merely express the hope that the unkind Italian proverb, 'Traduttore, traditore', will not be too often applied to me, and I trust that any reader who compares a page of Waldstein's Latin with my English version will at least realize my target: to recapture – in language which an intelligent young man might use in no very specific decade – the sense and spirit of these impressions of England under Elizabeth the First.

What I do wish to defend, however, or at least to explain, are the notes. They are meant for *every* interested reader, and the specialist historian is asked for his indulgence when such expressions as 'bezant', 'arquebus', and 'morning-star' are explained for the benefit of those who are less expert than himself. Furthermore, there is no reason why the most cultivated American or other non-English reader should know instinctively that it is not Edward III but the Black Prince who is buried in Canterbury Cathedral, that the Book in the Oxford University coat-of-arms has not two but seven seals,

---

* Chapman was the only translator who had enough spirit to say what he really thought about his critics: 'much less I weigh the frontless detractions of some stupid ignorants that . . . whisper behind me vilifying of my translation.'·

and that Theobalds was pronounced 'Tibbalds'. The explanations have been written for anyone – historian or non-specialist – who is genuinely interested to know the details about the people whom the young traveller met and the things and places which he saw. Some of these details are of importance, some are perhaps trivial, but the unimportant is by no means to be automatically equated with the uninteresting. I fully realize of course that there may be many serious-minded readers who care nothing for the fact that the stuffed bird of paradise which Waldstein saw at Windsor Castle was possibly a colourful but fraudulent sham constructed from parakeet feathers for the Chinese export market, but after all, an uninterested reader is under no obligation to read my notes and discover the opinion of the Curator of Birds at the London Zoo upon the subject: notes on this and on other trivia are included for the benefit of those who are interested in details and who like to have even incidental allusions checked and verified.

Any reference to 'trivialities' must of itself suggest the crucial question: 'What is the real historical value of a diary such as this?' From one point of view the truthful answer seems to be: 'Rather small.' Very few facts of historical importance appear in any foreign visitor's diary which cannot be discovered in greater detail from other and more authoritative sources. The Tudor historian is not likely to be impressed by the statement that the Earl of Mountjoy had 'recently been sent to Ireland' in summer 1600, or that the Governor of Dover Castle was 'a knight named Fane'. It has long been known that Mountjoy finally accepted the office of Lord Deputy (in succession to Essex) in November 1599 and that he left England in the following February; furthermore the historian can, if he wishes, quite easily prove himself more knowledgeable than the diarist by giving Sir Thomas Fane his Christian name.

The Diary does give us some hitherto unrecorded items of information about the contents of the Tudor palaces and their gardens. A few more of its facts (such as the treatment given to that nobly staunch English Papist with the six musical daughters) may perhaps find a place in some future social history of the period, but as we follow Waldstein's pages we begin to realize that isolated facts – the individual details of his picture – are only of minor importance. What really impresses us, and rightly, is the total picture itself: his whole panorama of tourist England in late Elizabethan times.

Like any foreign student-visitor of today, he sets out with his friends to see the sights: Canterbury Cathedral, Westminster Abbey, St Paul's, the Tower; Oxford and Cambridge; a few stately homes; Windsor Castle and Hampton Court. By the time we have read two pages we are completely 'en rapport' with him and bridge the centuries, seeing these places (and others now lost to us) through his eager interested eyes. We forgive him for copying out all those inscriptions from paintings and tombstones, and, with him, we too are awed and thrilled by Her Majesty at Greenwich, are impressed by the doctoral dissertations at Cambridge (and feel a shared sympathy at the scarlet mortification of one unfortunate don there); we visit the library at Oxford just recently restored by Thomas Bodley; we stare at the glories of Windsor and the treasures of Hampton Court, and, down at Rochester, go on board the *Elisabeth Jonas*, most splendid of the ships that, only twelve years ago, sailed out to engage the Spanish Armada.

Numerous other foreign visitors have given us their impressions of Elizabethan England. Waldstein, although at nineteen he was the youngest of these, is among the very best. It needed considerable charm and address (as well as his noble birth) to make so obviously good an impression upon Queen Elizabeth that 'she promised then and there that all the doors of her kingdom should be open to me', and a hint of that pleasing personality comes across in the Diary. Since first I met his manuscript I myself have found him a most excellent travelling companion.

# INTRODUCTION

*The Diary and the Diarist*  The Diary is a fat little parchment-bound book which measures only $6\frac{1}{4}$ by $4\frac{1}{4}$ inches. On its spine is a label inscribed 'Reg. lat. 666', and inside is written '282 n Pet' with the date 1656. Although the ink of the manuscript has browned and the pages are yellowed with age, there is little difficulty in reading the text, which is in Latin.

After some quotations from the Psalms and a prayer for God's guidance throughout his life, the diarist gives a brief résumé of his childhood years and schooldays, first at the famous Latin school at Iglau (now Jihlava) on the Bohemia-Moravia border, and then at Brieg (Brzeg) in Silesia. His name was Zdeněk Brtnický z Valdštejna, but he Latinizes this in the first page of the Diary as 'Zdenkonius Brtnicensis, Baro a Waldstein', and I have referred to him as 'Waldstein' throughout, as coming more trippingly on the Western European tongue than do his correct names and titles.

He had been born in 1581, and his father, Jindrich Brtnický z Valdštejna, had died when he was still a child. From his uncle Hynek, Chief Justice of Moravia, he had inherited the Budejovice estates at the age of fourteen, when the diary records: 'Anno 1595, 25 (vel 15) Octobris. Dominus Patruus meus per $ἐυθανασίαν$ migravit in $ἀθανασίαν$.' ('In the year 1595, on 25 (or 15) October, my lord uncle passed through a good death into everlasting life.') This entry and all other entries make use of both the Old Style and the new Gregorian calendars. The diarist abandoned the Old Style at the beginning of 1600.

Daily entries in the Diary begin on 1 January 1597, soon after the beginning of Waldstein's life as an undergraduate; he had matriculated at Strasbourg University (a popular seat of learning for the sons of Protestant families) at the age of fifteen in September 1596. During these student years Waldstein records very little except for the subjects of his daily studies, so that the entries for consecutive days are often identical, or nearly so:

[1598] 22 Feb, 4 Martii
              Versus Vergilii, Musica, Gallica lectio.
      23 Feb, 5 Martii
              Versus Vergilii, Musica, Gallica lectio.
      24 Feb, 6 Martii
              Scripsi literas ad d. patrem, Musica, Gallica lectio.

(The letter was written to his guardian, Charles the elder of Zerotin.) These pages are, with a few exceptions, repetitive and dull, and are likely to be of interest only to the specialist educational historian. One of the exceptions is a note of ten plays which he had seen performed by a troupe of English actors at the end of July and the beginning of August 1597. They were: *de quodam Duce Farrari, de Filio Perdito, de Zuzanna, de Fausto, de Esther, de quodam Viro quem defraudavit Diabolus, de Judith, de Judaeo Divite, de Sene, qui Oxori diffidebat*, and *de Errasto*. *Faustus* was probably Marlowe's (known to have been performed on the Continent); the others are not famous plays, and most are known only from lists like Waldstein's (see E. K. Chambers, *The Elizabethan Stage*, II, 1923, pp. 270ff.).

Soon after his eighteenth birthday Waldstein gave a farewell dinner and left Strasbourg for the travels which, with occasional intervals for study, were to occupy him for the next three years. From now on there is a marked change in his attitude to his Diary: what had been a comparatively prosaic record of lectures attended, and of dinner guests, becomes a detailed and most interesting account of his travels, giving us his readers an opportunity to see with him something of Renaissance Europe.

His method of keeping the Diary changed also. As a student he had merely written down – sometimes scrawled – the subjects which he had studied that day; now (it is easy to deduce from the Diary itself) he made rough notes on the spot and then wrote them up carefully when time allowed. An occasional error may creep in during this transcription: the hurried 7 is mistaken for a 2, and he even misread (his mind must have been wandering when he copied out folio 133) his own 'maximum' and wrote down 'marinum'. Also, the method of writing up notes some time after the event may produce a proleptic statement: on 7 July he saw the young Earl of Desmond in the Tower and at the same time reports (though inaccurately) his escape from there some four weeks later. During the English tour there was only one day in which he had enough leisure to be able to record 'Wrote up my Diary'; but in summer 1602, after his arrival home from Italy on 5 June, this entry occurs very frequently until 26 August, when he writes, doubtless with a feeling of duty done: 'Descriptionem itineris mei absolvi' – 'Finished the description of my journey.' He clearly intended the Diary to provide him in later life with a complete and detailed record of his youthful travels.

After leaving Strasbourg he made a tour through part of France and spent a few weeks at his studies in Paris. His next trip was to the Netherlands, where he spent two months seeing nearly all the cities of what is now Belgium and Holland. He returned to France for a period of study in Orleans (the occasional French phrase now slips into the Latin text: the farewell dinner which he gave to his friends there lasted 'Jusque 3 heures'); after this comes a journey to Provence, then north to the Loire, Chartres, Paris once more, and up to Calais for the English tour which is the subject of this book.

He returned, through Paris and Geneva, to Strasbourg in order to make his preparations for the last and longest tour, this time via Germany and Austria to Renaissance Italy. Through the pages of the Diary we visit all the major cities, for three and a half months follow his studies in Siena, and then take the road back to Moravia in 1602.

The Diary ends on the last day of 1603. The tone is cheerful: a few days previously the Count of Thurn had given a 'benevolum responsum' to Waldstein's request to marry his daughter Magdalena. A young man would naturally be glad to have his future father-in-law's consent, but unless Waldstein was quite unduly modest it can hardly have come as a surprise. We know nothing of his personal appearance, as unfortunately no portrait of him has survived, but he was nobly born, wealthy and the lord of large estates, sincere in his Protestant faith, and (we can fairly deduce from the Diary) intelligent and sociable. What more in a son-in-law could any girl's father require?

'Atque ita hic finit Annus 1603', he writes, and concludes the Diary with a short prayer.

The fate of the Diary became involved with the fate of the diarist himself. Magdalena of Thurn died in 1614, and as his second wife Waldstein married Katerina Křinecká of Ronov. Both the Thurn and the Křinecká families were prominent in the revolt of the mainly Protestant Moravian Estates against the militantly Catholic Archduke Ferdinand, and Waldstein himself vigorously supported the Protestant cause. When the Directorium was established in Moravia he became one of its twenty-nine members, and a few months later, in August 1619, when Frederick of the Palatinate (the unlucky Winter King, son-in-law of James I) was elected to the monarchy, Waldstein, as his Chamberlain, held an official post in the new royal Government.

Frederick did not remain King for long. In 1620 Ferdinand won a decisive victory at the Battle of the White Mountain. Forty-five of the most prominent revolutionaries were arrested and sentenced to death; of these, twenty-six were executed and the remainder (Waldstein among them) had their sentences commuted to life imprisonment and all their property confiscated. Waldstein was imprisoned in Spilberk

I   *A view into the Great Garden at Whitehall Palace – 'a most lovely garden; it has a number of pillars with figures of animals on them' (p. 59). The griffin, just visible to the left of the serving maid, was the heraldic beast of Edward III. In the distance to the south is the Clock House at Westminster (see the illustrations on pp. 38–39). (From a painting by an unknown artist, c. 1545. Reproduced by gracious permission of Her Majesty The Queen)*

II  Portrait of Edward VI as a child by Hans Holbein the Younger, 1539, which Waldstein saw at Whitehall (p. 47). (National Gallery of Art, Washington, Andrew W. Mellon Collection)

III  'Glittering with the glory of majesty and adorned with jewellery and precious gems', Queen Elizabeth appeared before Waldstein at Greenwich (p. 73). In this image, painted at about the time of Waldstein's visit, the Virgin Queen moves in triumph like an emperor. (From a picture attributed to Robert Peake. By courtesy of Simon Wingfield Digby, Esq., Sherborne Castle)

IV 'A copy of Cicero's "De Officiis" printed almost as soon as the printing press was invented' (p. 105): the opening of Book 2, decorated with the Prince of Wales's feathers for Prince Arthur. (Reproduced by kind permission of Emmanuel College, Cambridge)

Castle at Brno, and despite pleas for his release when he fell sick, he died there on 24 June 1623 at the age of 42.

With the confiscation of Waldstein's property many of his books, including the Diary, went to augment the magnificent collection of the Cardinal Archbishop Franz von Dietrichstein at Nikolsburg. During the Thirty Years War the Swedes invaded Moravia, and in 1645 Nikolsburg was captured; the Cardinal's books were seized as spoils of war and after two years were sent to the Royal Swedish Library in Stockholm.

In 1654 Queen Christina of Sweden abdicated. Her librarian Isaac Vossius included Waldstein's Diary among the many books which the Queen took with her, and in Antwerp, where she resided for a time, he settled down to the recataloguing of her manuscripts. Ex-Queen Christina then made her much-publicized entry into Rome under triumphal arches erected to do honour to the new convert. Vossius completed the cataloguing, dividing the manuscripts into two groups: the Petau collection (Petaviani) and the remainder (non-Petaviani). The Diary, Number 282 of the latter group, therefore carries the Vossius catalogue mark '282 n Pet' and the date 1656. The library followed the ex-Queen to Rome in 1657.

After Queen Christina's death in 1689 her library was acquired by Pope Alexander VIII, and since May 1690 the Diary has remained in the Vatican Library, catalogued as Reg. lat. 666, i.e. Number 666 of the Queen's Latin manuscripts.

(Professor J. V. Polišenský of the Charles University, Prague, and Mr Jiří Louda, the Czech heraldic artist, most kindly provided me with much useful information about the revolt of the Estates, and I am also indebted to Dr Christian Callmer and to Dr Uno Willers of the Royal Swedish Library for the details of the Diary's travels from Nikolsburg to Rome via Stockholm.)

*Other Diarists*

My notes on the Diary contain occasional quotations from other diarists of the period whose names may not be familiar to the general reader. Best of all the 'tourist descriptions' of Elizabethan England until now have been the accounts of Paul Hentzner in 1598, and of Thomas Platter in 1599. (Waldstein's, in 1600, completes this trio of distinguished diaries in consecutive years.)

Paul Hentzner, a lawyer of Brandenburg, came to England as companion to a young Silesian nobleman. His Diary, first published at Nuremberg in 1612, was translated by Richard Bentley and published by Horace Walpole from Strawberry Hill in 1757.

Thomas Platter, of Switzerland, who had studied medicine in Montpellier, visited England in autumn 1599. His Diary remained in manuscript for many years: it was then translated into English by Clare Williams and published in 1937.

Two other interesting accounts have been published by the Royal Historical Society. One is the Diary of Leopold von Wedel. His visit was in 1584 and – after his return from Scotland – in the spring of the following year. His descriptions are almost exclusively concerned with London. (See *Trans. Royal Hist. Soc.*, 1895.) The other account is that of the young Duke of Stettin-Pomerania, who visited England in 1602. It was written at his orders by his secretary, late tutor, Frederic Gerschow. (See *Trans. Royal Hist. Soc.*, 1892.)

Another secretary who wrote the travel diary of his master was Jacob Rathgeb, who visited England with Frederick, Duke of Württemberg, in 1592. The Duke, known in England as Count Mompelgard, had persistently begged Queen Elizabeth to honour him with the Order of the Garter. He is probably the original 'cozen Garmombles' of the Quarto *Merry Wives of Windsor*.

Rathgeb's description and those of the Duke's son, Louis Frederick (1610), Justus Zinzerling (*c.* 1610), Johann Ernest, Duke of Saxe-Weimar (1613), the Dane Peter Eisenberg (1614), and some others, are printed in W. B. Rye's *England as seen by Foreigners in the Days of Elizabeth and James I*, London, 1865 (reprinted New York, 1967).

Other foreign visitors include the Dane Thage Thott, who visited England in 1606 and whose Diary is in the Royal Library, Copenhagen, and the Frenchman L. Grenade, whose lively and informative *Les Singularitez de Londres* was written in 1578 and found its way, like Waldstein's Diary, to the Vatican via Queen Christina's collection.

*The Mechanics of the Translation*

Waldstein's text is represented as closely as possible: in general, mistakes are left *in situ* and are corrected only in the notes. I have, however, disregarded mis-spellings in the Latin as well as some odd renderings of English place-names, such as Grenewicz for Greenwich, Nonsuttz for Nonsuch, etc. Some of Waldstein's inaccuracies were probably due to a misunderstanding of his informant's Latin. This was a not uncommon difficulty, as Latin was pronounced differently in England: Coryat in 1618 discovered that until he had adjusted his pronunciation to Continental practice his Latin was almost unintelligible abroad: 'The Italian when he uttereth any Latin word wherein this letter i is to be pronounced long, doth alwaies pronounce it as a double e, viz. ee. As for example he pronounceth feedes for fides: veeta for vita: ameecus for amicus &c. ... Neither is it proper to Italy only but to all other nations whatsoever in Christendome saving to England.'

In his essay 'On Education' Milton advocated changing the English pronunciation to conform with usage abroad, but his advice was not followed until Latin had already ceased to be a *lingua franca*. When Thomas Platter visited Eton he found: 'I could not discover a single student able to talk to me in Latin, they all pointed to their mouths with their fingers and shook their heads.' Platter clearly thought them ignorant, but the Etonians could probably have conversed with him well enough if he had adjusted his pronunciation to theirs.

I have not altered dates, although Waldstein used the then-new Gregorian Calendar instead of the Old Style Calendar which persisted in England right up to 1751. To adjust for this, subtract ten days from each date, leaving the day of the week unchanged, so that Saturday 8 July becomes Saturday 28 June.

With titles I have been faithful to the original, which is why Queen Elizabeth's royal father appears on folio 173v both as 'Henry the Eighth' and 'Henry VIII'. Waldstein sometimes used Arabic and sometimes Roman numerals for such titles, but here I prefer to be consistent and have substituted 'Edward III' for his 'Edward 3', etc. All the brackets are where Waldstein put them: I have not inserted any of my own.

Latin verses often appear, and verse does demand that the translator be an arbiter between the sometimes antagonistic demands of precise translation and poetic style. Sir Richard Burton of the *Arabian Nights*, who turned much Eastern poetry into English verse, expressed the feelings of most translators when he commented upon the difficulty of drawing the line between 'unendurable inaccuracy' and 'intolerable servility'. I myself have inclined towards a certain amount of 'servility' to the meaning of the Latin verses which the Diary records, because such verses are far more likely to be of interest for their content than for the way in which they have been Englished. When reluctantly discarding some line or phrase which pleased me in favour of a less attractive but more accurate version, I bore in mind (as a fairly effective antidote to temptation) F. L. Lucas' sardonic but well-justified remark that Omar Khayyam's *Rubaiyat* was 'not rendered into verse by Fitzgerald – it was *sur*rendered'.

The reader will notice that occasionally a piece of verse has been translated into prose. This has occurred when my attempts at verse

INTRODUCTION

have, for one reason or another, seemed unsatisfactory. I found, for instance, that I was incapable of putting the lines about Henry VIII and the Emperor Charles V on folio 178v into any sort of verse which was not, in my opinion, just faintly risible and out of keeping with the neat epigrammatic tone of the original. If one of my readers can do better I shall be delighted to substitute his lines for my own and to echo Tom Coryat's imperturbable and praiseworthy comment: 'If though dost, (learned reader) thy capacity is more pregnant than mine.'

*The Notes*  Robert Graves, in his Introduction to *The Greek Myths*, writes: 'an educated person is now no longer expected to know (for instance) who Deucalion, Pelops, Daedalus, Oenone, Laocoön, or Antigone may have been'. He is perfectly correct in this, but it is impossible to mark the place where common knowledge leaves off and classical learning begins. Quite arbitrarily, I have assumed that references to Tarquin and Lucretia, to Prometheus, and to the Labours of Hercules need no explanations, but have also assumed that readers may very well be vague or ignorant about Ixion, Scaevola, and Marcus Curtius.

I have preferred not to lengthen the notes with such statements of failure as I might well have written right at the start: 'No record exists at the Maritime Museum in Amsterdam or at the Public Record Office at The Hague (or in their counterparts in Antwerp) of Captain Cornelis van den Bricsen and his ship.' Numerous such gaps remain: I have pointed out a few, but others are obvious, and I should be very grateful for any information which would fill them.

Experts in very varied fields have taken time and trouble in answering my many queries, and I am glad to express my gratitude for so great an amount of generous help. More detailed thanks will be found in the notes themselves.

*Bibliography*  Jeanne Odier (now Signora Bignami) wrote by far the most generally informative article on Waldstein and his Diary in 'Voyage en France d'un jeune Morave, 1599–1600', published in *Mélanges d'Archéologie et d'Histoire* (XLIII, Rome, 1926). This gives details of Waldstein's experiences in France and also a description of the contents of the Diary with an outline of the diarist's career.

Those pages of the Diary which deal with Waldstein's tour of the Netherlands were published in Latin by J. A. F. Orbaan, in *Beschieden in Italie* (I, The Hague, 1911, pp. 170–78).

Another article by Dr Orbaan on the Diary is 'Deutsche Kunststädte und Deutsche Kunstsammlungen um 1600', in *Zeitschrift für Museumskunde* (XIII, Berlin, 1917). He gives a general description of the Diary and quotes the Latin text of Waldstein's account of Stuttgart, Augsburg, and Innsbruck, towns through which the diarist passed en route for Italy.

The only article which deals exclusively with the English tour was written by O. Odložilík and published in *Časopis Matice Moravske* (Brno, 1935, pp. 280–88). It provides a detailed account of the places in England which Waldstein visited and the people whom he met.

B. Dudik's *Iter Romanum* (Vienna, 1855, p. 232) also gives a brief description of the Diary. It is very uninformative about the English tour.

F. Hrubý's *Etudiants tchèques aux écoles protestantes de l'Europe occidentale à la fin du 16e et au début du 17e siècle* (Purkyne University, Brno) includes some letters written by Waldstein and to him during his student days.

Hrubý's *Moravská Korespondence a Akta* (I, Brno, 1934) contains letters pleading for Waldstein's release from prison when he was too sick to leave his bed, so that he could be cared for by his wife.

The standard Czech encyclopaedia, *Ottův Slovník Naučný*, has an article on the family with a section on the diarist himself (stating, incidentally, that he died in 1624 rather than 1623).

An important collection of documents of the period which casts light on the people and places Waldstein saw is the Hatfield House Papers. I have drawn chiefly on material covered by vol. x of the *Calendar of the Manuscripts of the Most Hon. the Marquis of Salisbury* (London, 1904); my quotations are by courtesy of the Marquis of Salisbury. I have also to thank Mr R. H. Harcourt Williams, Archivist to the Marquis, for much kind help and useful information.

For the works of art and furnishings mentioned by Waldstein, an invaluable source of enlightenment is Sir Oliver Millar's edition of *The Inventories and Valuations of the King's Goods, 1649–51* (Walpole Society, London, 1972). The lists made on the order of Oliver Cromwell record the contents of each palace before they were dispersed. Sometimes they merely confirm Waldstein's text; at other times they supplement it. I have frequently drawn on Sir Oliver's book in my notes, where it is referred to as 'Millar, *Inventories*'.

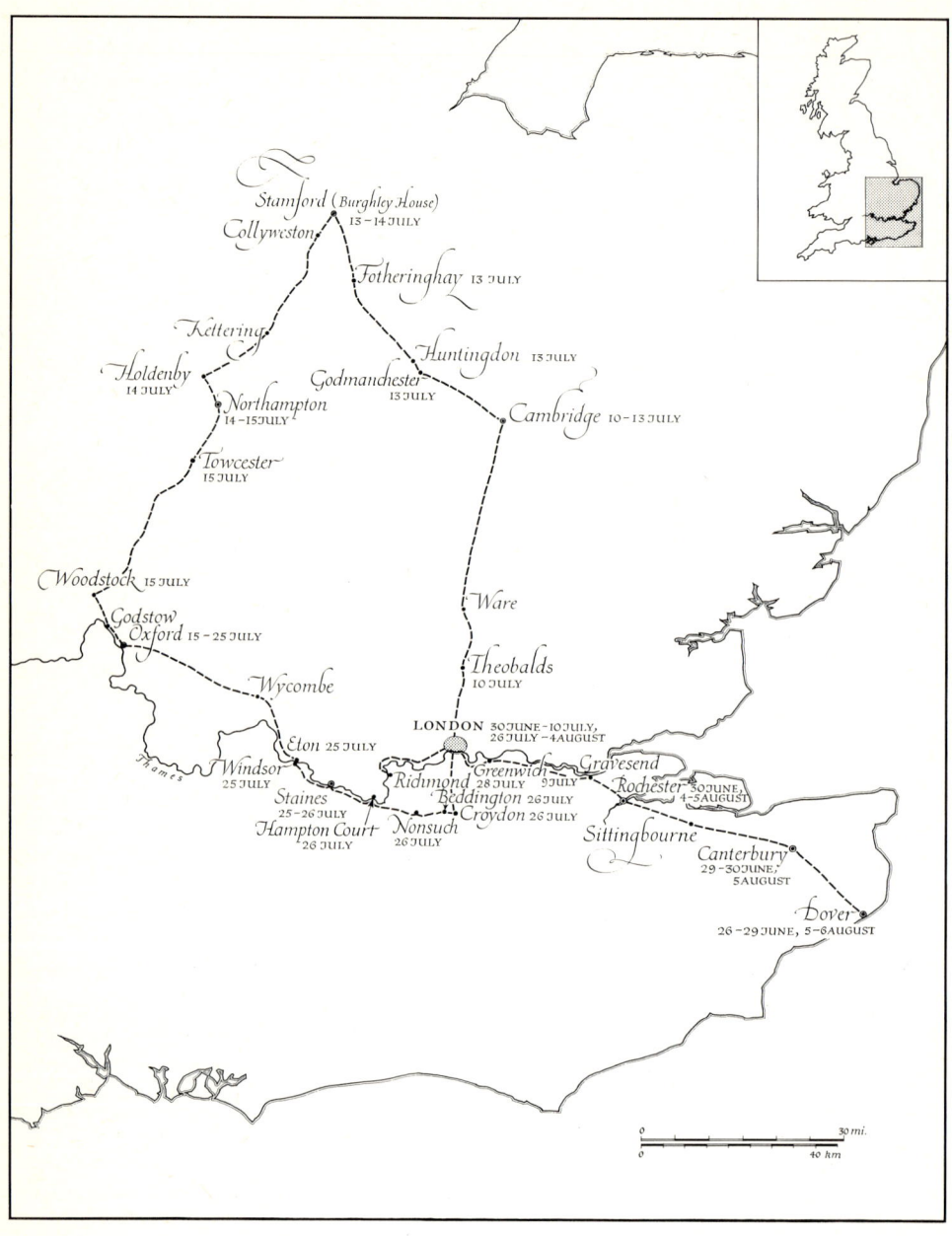

*Map showing the route of Waldstein's tour, with the dates when places are described. (Drawn by Hanni Bailey)*

\*A marginal reference in italics, preceded by 'f.', indicates the approximate beginning of a new folio in the manuscript of the Diary.

1  A number of differing lengths for a 'mile' were then in use on the Continent. Here Waldstein was using not the standard measurement of his own country (the 'medium Bohemian mile' of 9.25 km) but the 'short German mile' of 8,000 paces or 5.92 km. Seven 'short German miles' gives the correct distance of 41.44 km, i.e. just over 25 English miles from Calais to Dover harbour. (See Karel Kuchar, *Early Maps of Bohemia, Moravia and Silesia*, Prague, 1961.)

   While travelling through England Waldstein gives distances in English miles.

2  Sir Thomas Fane continued in office as Lieutenant of Dover Castle until at least 1606: a charter of that year names him as assistant to the Lord Warden of the Cinque Ports.

3  The Domestic State Papers contain no record of this restriction. It was probably found to be impracticable, and it certainly did not last long, for a letter from Fane to Sir Robert Cecil, Secretary to the Queen, dated 11 July Old Style (Hatfield House Papers, x, p. 230) shows that within a week foreign visitors were being sent on to London to report to the authorities there instead of being kept waiting at Dover: 'This forenoon there arrived from Calais divers gentlemen of Germany whose names I enclose. I have willed them to repair to you with this letter.'

   One of the names is 'Joachimus Ernestus Baro a Sonnenburg'. 'Baron Sonnenburg' was the pseudonym of the Margrave of Brandenburg, who, still travelling incognito, accompanied Waldstein back to the Continent.

4  Prince Ulrik (1578–1624), a younger brother of King Christian IV, is known to have visited England and Scotland in 1599, but the Royal Danish Library could produce no evidence that his stay in England was incognito.

## Sunday, 25 June

Had supper, and at 9 o'clock sailed from Calais in a fine ship, a Dutch armed vessel; M. de Pailly, the United Provinces representative, had arranged the passage for us with the ship's captain, Cornelis van den Bricsen. The sea was so utterly calm that we could have made the crossing in no more than a skiff; this was unfortunate, however, as it made for a much slower journey.

## Monday, 26 June

Because of this it was about noon today when, with the wind already freshening against us, we reached the headland and harbour of Dover (10 miles, though some reckon it 7, from Calais).

Dover

This is one of the chief ports of England: it is situated in Kent, and has a strongly fortified castle high up on a hill commanding both the sea and the town. A knight called Fane is its present Governor.

We went up here first, which is the rule for persons entering the country, and we each paid 4 *denarii* ('pennies' they call them: 12 are equal to 10 French *sous* in value; this payment is called 'tavern-gold') and after this we had to give our names to the Magistrates and to the town governor or 'Mayor'.

We had intended to ride off after lunch that same day, but then all our hopes and plans were upset: we were detained by the Magistrates under some new regulation, the first time it had ever been enforced. According to one story this was because the King of Denmark's brother had recently gone for a tour through the country incognito and had failed to pay his respects to the

5 The Archduke Maximilian (1558–1618) was the brother of Rudolph II, Holy Roman Emperor and King of Germany. Rowland Whyte wrote to Sir Robert Sidney on 14 June 1600: 'here were at Court to see the Queen some high Germans, amongest them, it is thought, came disguised the Archduke Maximilian, who went for a Gentleman of Silesia'. (Sidney Papers: *Report on the Manuscripts of Lord de L'Isle and Dudley*, II, ed. C. L. Kingsford, London, 1934, p. 210.)

6 I have not discovered any reference in English documents to the odd behaviour of these Austrian visitors. They had clearly provoked suspicion of an attempt to poison the royal dishes.

7 Waldstein was understandably prejudiced against Dover; he gains some support however from Paul Hentzner, who wrote unappreciatively that the town 'is more famous for the convenience of its port ... than for either its elegance or populousness'.

Queen; another version made it Maximilian, the Emperor's brother, who was responsible. We heard the true reason afterwards, however, when we were in London: it was actually because of three Austrians (men whom we ourselves had known quite well when we were in Orleans) who shortly before our arrival had been admitted to the Queen's Palace. Then, before they had looked at anything at all except for the kitchens, they had suddenly disappeared or rather had bolted hot-foot. The Queen was very much put out by this, and – suspecting I don't know what – she gave strict orders to her officials and to the Port Authorities in particular, that no persons, especially those of noble or illustrious birth, were to be allowed to enter the country unless their names had first been noted and submitted to the Palace.

That then was the reason why we were forced to spend not just this one day but also – and in utter frustration – Tuesday the 27th, Wednesday the 28th, and half of the 29th of June as well in dismal idleness at Dover, not only throwing away our time in such a dull place but wasting our money as well; and this we had already been forced to pay out lavishly and not without a good deal of ill-feeling, to the Dunkirk inn-keeper's wife who swindled us so.

### Thursday, 29 June

In the morning we went to the Governor of the Castle and absolutely begged him for permission to leave, but he still put us off for another day; however, just as we were about to have lunch he sent his servant with better news than we had even hoped for, saying that although he had not yet received a reply from the Court (actually

8  A number of other visitors expressed surprise at the speed of English horses. Hentzner wrote: 'We took post-horses for London; it is surprising how swiftly they run', and Thomas Platter, travelling from Gravesend to Dover, is more specific about their pace. He writes of his companions: 'Many of them experienced great discomfort from the posts because of the small saddles which they had to ride without post cushions, and all made great speed, so that we covered the 44 English miles in about 5 hours.'

9  This was quite true. Durovernum (Canterbury) was a town of some size, and its theatre is the largest to have been discovered in Britain.

10  Canterbury had a substantial Huguenot population, and church services in French were held in the large Romanesque crypt of the Cathedral from 1574 until 1897, since when they have been held in the Black Prince's chantry chapel. (I have to thank Miss A. M. Oakley, the Diocesan Archivist, for this and other information about the Cathedral.)

11  The Archbishop's income in 1600 was largely derived from rents. Its exact amount is not known, but the Librarian at Lambeth Palace considers that Waldstein's figure is a likely one.

12  Hales died in 1589: he was Treasurer of the unsuccessful counter-attack expedition against the Spaniards in the year after the Armada. His memorial, with its relief sculpture showing his body being committed to the sea, can still be seen in the Cathedral.

13  Lady Margaret Holland and her two successive husbands, John Beaufort, Earl of Somerset, and Thomas Plantagenet, Duke of Clarence. Two years before her death in 1439 Lady Margaret gave heraldic glass for the windows of the Warriors' Chapel where she and her husbands now lie. Coats-of-arms of the Holland family can be seen in the south window.

14  William Lovelace, Serjeant at Law, High Steward of the Liberties of Christ Church. His tomb no longer exists. In the last line of his epitaph 'vive' should almost certainly read 'vivo', and I have so translated.

> Lo, happily did I discard my body's heavy weight,
> And in exchange for lasting bliss, far lesser goods I give.
> For since the law of Heaven, the unyielding course of Fate
> Debars me from my earthly life, now with my God I live.

we did not believe this) yet as we had begged so earnestly for his help he would give us permission to continue our journey, and that he had at the same time arranged to have a letter of introduction prepared for us.

This was most welcome news. So we lunched, and after spending some time in arguing with our very grasping landlady, we hired horses – each one a real Pegasus – and mounted, and covered with dust and sweat we reached *Cantuaria* (known here as Canterbury) in 2½ hours, 12 English miles from Dover.

Canterbury is a very ancient town which was important even in Roman times. It is chiefly famous for its cathedral, which is particularly large and splendid, and which contains numerous marble tombs; underneath it there is another church where they hold services in French and get congregations of some 2,000 people. The church is dedicated to Christ, and it is extremely well endowed, for its bishop receives an annual income of 10,000 pounds sterling, the equivalent of 33,333 crowns.

One of the chapels contains a memorial to an illustrious knight named James Hales; nearby are the tombs of two earls and a countess, whose names can be read in one of the windows. In the choir a doctor of laws called Lovelace is buried; he has the following epitaph:

*En ego sum felix carnis qui mole solutus*
*Mutavi aeternis deteriora bonis.*
*Nam cum me rerum series fixus, Deorum*
*Ordo vetat Mundo vivere: vive Deo.*

Further down the choir is the tomb of Edward, King of England, with the inscription:

15 The Black Prince never lived to succeed his father as king. He captured the King of France at the Battle of Poitiers in 1356. His armour is still on display: it was probably made especially for his funeral procession. The sword was stolen long ago and has never been recovered.

The inscription reads correctly: 'Cy gist le Noble Prince Mons Edward aisnez filz du tres Noble Roy Edward Tiers: Prince d'Aquitane & de Gales, Duc de Cornwalle, & Comte de Cestre, qui morust, en le feste de la Trinite, questoit le VIII jour de Juin, l'an de grace mil trois centz septante sisine, Lalme de qui Dieu eut mercy. Amen.' In Waldstein's transcript, '(N)' stands for 'name'.

16 Odet de Coligny, Cardinal de Chatillon (1517–71), had come to England almost certainly in connection with the Protestant cause, to which he was a convert. Waldstein is wrong in describing him as the French ambassador. There is no evidence of his having been poisoned, but anti-Catholic feeling would have kept the story alive (it is stated, for instance, in John Dart's *History and Antiquities of the Cathedral Church of Canterbury*, London, 1726).

Coligny's tomb was intended to be temporary, pending the return of his body to France, and it remains a very bleak structure without inscription or ornament of any kind.

17 William Bruchelle was not a bishop but a judge. His death mask has not survived.

18 This painting no longer exists.

19 St Augustine's Chair, of Purbeck marble, dates from the thirteenth century.

20 This mosaic, of the type known as *opus alexandrinum*, is in the floor of the Trinity Chapel. It dates from *c*. 1220 and is all that is left of the once magnificent shrine of St Thomas, destroyed in 1539.

21 A slip of the pen for Thomas a Becket. Waldstein was far too well educated to be seriously confused about the identities of the two famous saints.

He is incorrect in stating that the site of Becket's shrine was the place of his murder. The crime was committed in the north-west transept.

22 The brass was that of Simon Islip, Archbishop of Canterbury 1349–66 and Fellow of Merton College, Oxford, a Doctor of Civil and Canonical Law.

Dart quotes the inscription with the comment that the tomb was then (1726) defaced; it was later removed. Dart's version differs from Waldstein's in that he gives the lines in a slightly different order and adds two more at the end. He also reads 'Islip' for 'ille' (l.1), 'seno' for 'deno' (l.5), and 'e feno' for 'e freno' (l.8). These three readings are obviously correct and I have followed them in my translation. 'Simon, Prince of Pastors' is Simon Peter, from whom the Apostolic Succession is traced.

> Simon, a native of Islip, skilled both as a national jurist
> And in canonical law, now lies enclosed in this shelter
> As in the womb before birth. In this town, beloved by his clergy
> And by the whole of the realm, he held the place of Archbishop.
> Then, on the sixth of May, in the seventeenth year of his office
> In thirteen sixty-six, his bonds with the body were broken,
> With a cry:
>   'The flower is falling, it drops from the stem that is withered,
>   Him do I seek on high, Who lives in the glory of Heaven.'
> Simon, Prince of Pastors, grant to this Simon thy favour,
> May he attain, through their prayers, the fellowship of the apostles.

*Cy gist noble prince Eduard aisne fils du tresnoble Roy (N) frere jadis prince d'Aquitaine et de Gaules, Duc de Karnel et Conte de Cestre, qui mourut a la feste de la Trinite, qui etoit le 8 de Juin l'an de grace 1376.*

It was he who took the King of France prisoner, and because of this his helmet, sword, and other arms are displayed.

The tomb of King Henry IV of England and of his Queen is to be seen here, and here also lies the body of the Ambassador of the King of France, Cardinal Chatillon, who died of poison in England. We saw too the tomb of Bishop William Bruchelle together with his death mask which is most beautifully made. By the entrance to the choir is a fine painting of the story of the Revelation.

The choir is shut off by screens of wrought iron, and half-way along this choir stands the marble chair upon which the archbishops are enthroned. At the far end of the choir there is a piece of mosaic work done in marble: this is the place where Thomas Aquinas was murdered; his body for a long time lay in a raised tomb right at the end of the choir and was held in great reverence, but it has now been removed. In this church even the hangings are of cloth of gold.

A brass memorial in the nave has these lines:

> *Simon ille oriens, vir bina lege probatus*
> *Ut nascens moriens sic nunc jacet arcte ligatus,*
> *Arcem qui tenuit hic quondam pontificatus*
> *Clero quique fuit toti regno quoque gratus,*
> *Mil: trecenteno sexageno modo deno*
> *Eius septeno pastoratus quoque deno,*
> *Hic Maii seno rupto carnis voce freno:*
> *Flos cadit e freno, coelo peto qui sit amoeno*
> *Princeps pastorum fac Simon Apostolicorum*
> *Simon ut ille chorum per eos attingat eorum.*

23 The tomb, in the Warriors' Chapel, is that of the famous thirteenth-century Archbishop Stephen Langton; he is not known to have made any Biblical translations, but was responsible for the division of the Bible into chapters.

24 Canterbury, Sittingbourne, Rochester and Gravesend were the normal post stages for the Dover–London journey. Zinzerling, whose journey was made c. 1610, writes: 'Riding post from Dover to Canterbury costs three English shillings: from Canterbury to Sittingbourne the same: from Sittingbourne to Rochester about two shillings and sixpence: and from there to Gravesend one shilling and sixpence.'
  Travelling with such a frequent change of horses could be quite speedy. A letter dated 25 February 1600 from the Lieutenant of Dover Castle to Court, which was *not* marked, as Sir Thomas Fane sometimes marked urgent letters, 'hast post hast post hast hast with spede', is endorsed: 'Dover, 25 Feb., 3 afternoon; Canterbury, 6 afternoon; Sittingbourne, 8 at night; ... Dartford, 26 Feb., 6 in the morning.' (Hatfield House Papers, X, p. 43.)

25 This was a well-known inn. Platter also stayed there: 'turned in at a hostelry called the Fleur-de-Lys in Mark Lane, kept by a Frenchman, M. Briard'.

26 Lescinsky was an acquaintance from Moravia; he is mentioned earlier in the Diary, before Waldstein's arrival in England.

27 The whole of this description of London is taken from *Britannia*, by the antiquary William Camden, first published in 1586. Waldstein quotes Camden a number of times in his Diary, using the original Latin text.

*London, stretching like 'a bent bow or a crescent moon' from the Tower at the east of the City to the Abbey at the south-west of Westminster, and across London Bridge to Southwark, with its bull and bear pits. Waldstein lodged in Mark Lane, just north-west of the Tower. (From Braun and Hogenberg's 'Civitates Orbis Terrarum', 1572, based on drawings of c. 1560)*

In the chapel which I mentioned previously we were shown the tomb of a man named Stephen, who made the first translation of the Bible into French.

### Friday, 30 June

Early in the day we hired horses and leaving Canterbury behind us in 12 miles reached Sittingbourne. Pushing on from here at a good speed we completed the third and — by just a little — the shortest stage of our journey (actually a distance of about 10 miles), and arrived at Rochester within an hour. From Rochester we went on to Gravesend where the boat leaves, and we reckoned this as our half-way post.

Reached Gravesend at about midday, and after a light lunch boarded a small boat which brought us into London (12 miles away) three hours before sunset. Then we made for the French hostelry the Fleur-de-Lys, met Lescinsky, and felt not at all sorry to be spending some days in the city.

London (called 'Londres' by the French) is the capital of Great Britain, the seat of Britain's government, and the official residence of the Kings of England. It lies in the county of Middlesex, and is famous not only for its size but also as a meeting-place of different nations. It has great natural advantages from the two elements: it is sited on a fertile soil in which everything grows easily, and on a slope which rises gently beside the Thames. This placid river is a centre of trade for everything the world has to offer: at regular intervals it swells with the surge of Ocean's waves, and through its well-traversed channel, deep and wide enough for vessels of any size, it bears in daily such a store of the riches of the East and the West

28 The indisputably greatest trade centre was Venice.

29 Rendered as follows in Philemon Holland's English translation of Camden's *Britannia*, published in 1610:

> Along both bankes outstreched farre the City London lies
> Resembling much her mother Troie, aloft she lifts her eies,
> Whiles on a gentle rising hill she beareth towards East:
> A City pleasant for her site, in aire and soile much blest.
> Religious and populous: and hence she looks on hie
> And well deserves for to be cal'd the Britans Britanie.
> For learning, new Lutetia, Ormus for trade and wealth,
> A second Rome for valiant men, Chrysae for plate and health.

30 Ammianus Marcellinus, Book 27, VIII, 7; Tacitus, *Annals*, XIV, 33.

31 A menagerie had been established at the Tower of London in 1235 when Henry III was presented with three leopards by the Emperor Frederick II. The royal menagerie remained there until 1834 when the beasts were removed to the new Zoological Gardens in Regent's Park. The animals were housed in the barbican, which was commonly known as the Lion Tower until its demolition in the nineteenth century.

I have to thank Dr Alan Borg, formerly of the Tower Armouries, who kindly gave me this and much other detailed information about the Tower and its contents in Elizabethan times. (See also his 'Monkey Business at the Tower', *Country Life*, 26 May 1977.) Grenade, in *Les Singularitez de Londres* (1578), refers to the menagerie in the section dealing with 'la Tour': 'En une grosse et large tour qui est a l'entrée du premier dongeon de la dite Tour sont les Affricanes de sa ma$^{te}$. Entre lesquelles sont six ou sept que lions que lionnes, ieunes ou vieils: un liepard excellentement moucheté: un Porcepy, et un loup: qui est chose bien rare car on n'en voit point en tout le pays si on ne les nourrit expressement.'

that it now vies for second place among the trade centres of the Christian world: it provides a perfectly safe – and at the same time beautiful – anchorage for shipping, and is so thick on all sides with the masts and sails of vessels that one might imagine it a closely entwined forest.

Fully justified was the poet who praised the city in the following lines:

> *Londinium gemino procurrit litore longe*
> *Aemula maternae tollens sua lumina Troiae,*
> *Clementer surgente jugo dum tendit in ortum:*
> *Urbs peramoena situ, coeloque soloque beata,*
> *Urbs pietate potens, numeroso cive superba*
> *Urbsque Britannorum condigna Britannia dici;*
> *Quae nova doctrinis Lutetia, mercibus Ormus,*
> *Altera Roma viris, Chrysaea secunda metallis.*

Ammianus Marcellinus 1,200 years ago refers to the town as an ancient one, and Cornelius Tacitus in the time of Nero records that it was well-famed for the number of its merchants and for the extent of its commerce. Its longitude is 51 degrees 34", its latitude 25 degrees. The shape of the city is that of a bent bow or of a crescent moon.

## JULY

### Saturday, 1 July

As we were tired after our journey we had a quiet day in London and spent the time in lively and interesting conversation. (A group of thieves and robbers on their way to be hanged made a notable sight.)

### Sunday, 2 July

Attended Divine Service in French. In the afternoon we visited a place where we saw three great lions and two

32 Platter, Hentzner and Grenade all mention the porcupine. The Diary reads 'erinaceum marinum', a *sea* porcupine. The phrase mystified me at first, but as Waldstein's 'r' and 'x' are almost indistinguishable from one another I realized that 'marinum' was merely a miscopying from his own on-the-spot notes of 'maximum' and – since this is a misspelling rather than a genuine error – I have translated it as such.

The whole question of 'translator's ethics' is a tricky one. If, for instance, a writer should mis-spell the word 'friend' by omitting the second letter, should a conscientious scholar translate the word as 'devil'? One's immediate (and perhaps correct) reaction is probably 'Nonsense!', but, all the same, it just *might* have been a Freudian slip, and be therefore significant. Each case, I feel, must be judged on its merits.

33 The phrase 'uxores aurifabrorum' appears elsewhere in the Diary. Its different contexts suggest that it is an expression of the highest praise: we can assume that at the Tower Zoo, or on the way home, he saw 'three entrancingly attractive young women'. Hitherto no classical scholar whom I have met has ever come across the expression 'goldsmith's wife' as a synonym of beauty: it may have a private family joke; or it may possibly have been derived from Jane Shore, mistress of Edward IV, who was known as a goldsmith's wife, and was celebrated in Elizabethan literature.

34 This is easily the most exasperating entry in the whole Diary. No name is given either to the theatre visited or to the play, which might have identified the theatre. (He uses the word 'comoediam', but the expression was loosely used and could quite well apply to any sort of play.) What follows may be a first-hand description of Shakespeare's Globe Theatre in the year after it was built, but there is not enough evidence here to distinguish it from the Rose or the Swan. The Globe was not only the newest, it was also the most splendid of the theatres of its time, and the most probable theatre for a wealthy young foreigner to visit is the newest and the best.

These lines are the only ones in the Diary which are generally known; they are quoted by Sir Edmund Chambers in *The Elizabethan Stage* (II, London, 1923, p. 366) and are familiar to all serious students of the Elizabethan theatre. Chambers got his quotation from a letter to *The Times* (11 April 1914) written by an English resident in Rome who had attended a lecture given by Dr J. A. F. Orbaan who was engaged in research in the Vatican Library. The letter stated that the theatre was the Globe: the writer was obviously quoting Orbaan himself, who made the same statement in a learned periodical a few years later, as also did Odložilík, but neither had any evidence to support the claim. (For articles on the Diary by Orbaan and Odložilík, see my Bibliography, pp. 20–21.)

35 Almost every diarist comments upon the intriguing sight of the traitors' heads stuck upon poles above the bridge. Hentzner writes: 'We counted above thirty.' Platter is the most specific and states: 'Their descendants are accustomed to boast of this themselves, even pointing out to one their ancestors' heads on this same bridge, believing that they will be esteemed the more because their antecedents were of such high descent that they could even covet the crown.'

36 The Court of Justice was Westminster Hall, which for many centuries was the major English court of law. It was originally built by William Rufus but was entirely remodelled by Richard II and given its magnificent hammerbeam roof which is generally considered to be the finest piece of medieval timber-work in England. Soon after its completion Richard II stood trial there himself.

The Palace was the seat of the House of Lords and House of Commons and of lesser law courts. It stood on the site of the Houses of Parliament.

37 The book was Camden's *Reges &c. Westmonasterii sepulti*, an early example of a tourist's guide book. It had been first published that year, and Camden's presentation copy to Queen Elizabeth can be seen in the British Library.

32 lionesses, a leopard, a tiger, and a huge porcupine.
33 (Note: three wives of goldsmiths.)

### Monday, 3 July
Went to see an English play. The theatre follows the ancient Roman plan: it is built of wood and is so designed that the spectators can get a comfortable view of everything that happens in any part of the building.

On the way back we crossed the bridge; it has very fine buildings on it, and fixed to one of them can still be seen the heads of a number of earls and other noblemen who have been executed for treason.

### Tuesday, 4 July
Out for a walk and went inside St Paul's Cathedral, which I shall describe later.

### Wednesday, 5 July
Went along the Thames to the small town of Westminster. Although it is over a mile from the City, we went past buildings the whole way. The place gets its name from being situated on the western side of the City, and it is famous for its Abbey, its Court of Justice, and its Palace.

The Abbey, one of the finest in the whole of England, is most magnificent and also very beautiful; it is renowned as the place of the coronation of the Kings of England and as their place of burial. It contains a large number of chapels and some very splendid royal monuments: with reference to these, consult a special book, which is printed in London.

# LONDON

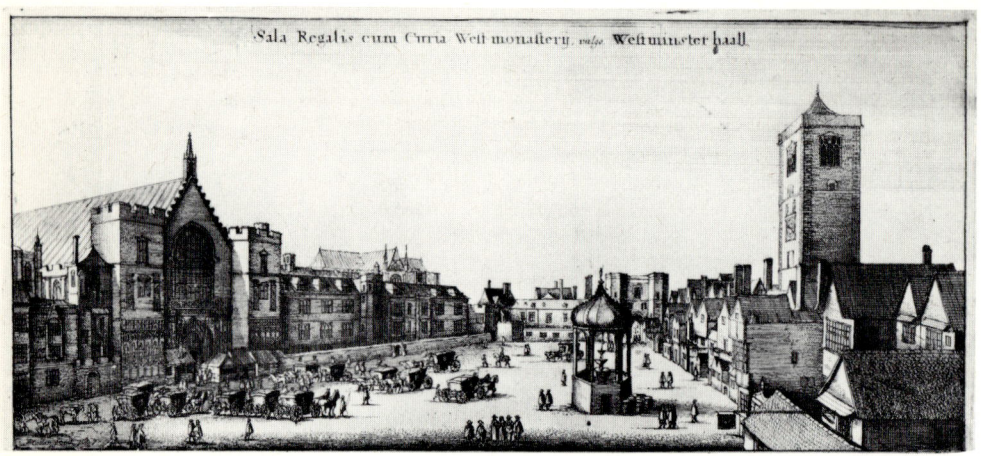

New Palace Yard, Westminster, seen from the present site of Big Ben. On the left is Westminster Hall, on the right the Clock House, and in the centre the fountain that flowed with wine at coronations. (Etching by the Bohemian artist Wenceslaus Hollar, 1647. British Museum, London)

(left) A London theatre, drawn about 1596 by another foreign visitor: the Swan, after Johannes de Witt, who noted – as Waldstein did when he visited a theatre – that 'its form resembles that of a Roman work'. (University Library, Utrecht, MS 842, f. 132r)
(above) Looking from Southwark across London Bridge to the City. Bridge Gate, at the far right, displays traitors' heads on poles. (From Visscher's panorama of 1616, based on drawings of c. 1600. Museum of London)

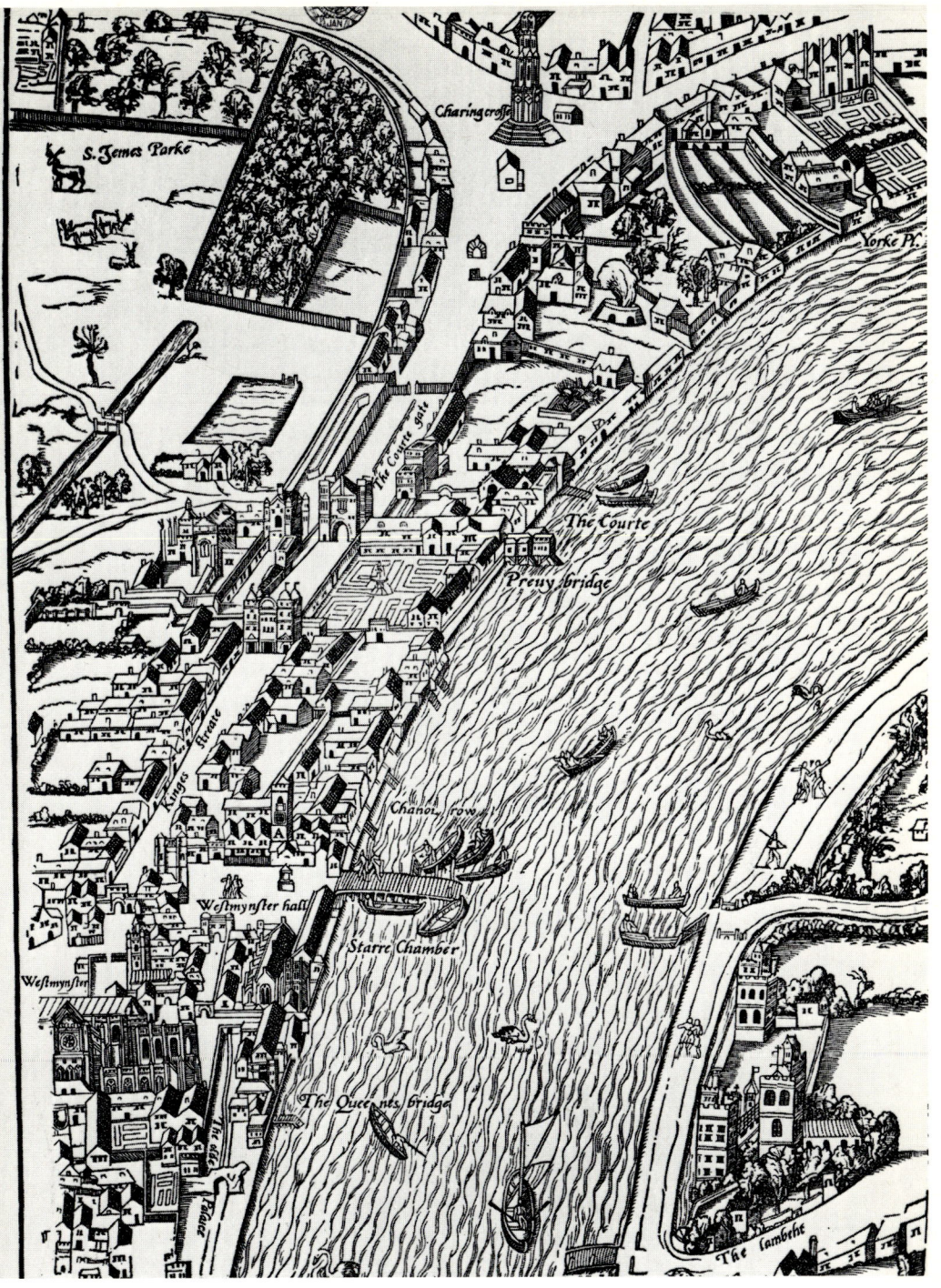

*Westminster, from Charing Cross down to the Abbey. North of the Abbey are Westminster Hall and the open-air fountain (see opposite, above). Further north, at the end of King Street, stands the complex of Whitehall Palace with its two great gates and large formal garden between them and the river (see colour plate I). To the north-west is St James's Park, to the south-east, across the river, Lambeth Palace. (From Vertue's eighteenth-century copy of 'Civitas Londinum', which he attributed to Ralph Agas, probably based on maps of c. 1560)*

38 'Marble throne' is incorrect: the Coronation Chair is of wood. Waldstein is also wrong when he goes on to say that it had come from Scotland: he seems to have misunderstood the word 'seat' in Camden's sentence ('After defeating the Scots ...'), which he quotes verbatim. The seat upon which the Scottish kings were crowned is the Stone of Destiny, or Stone of Scone: Edward I had seized it, and had the Coronation Chair made c. 1300 to contain it.

39
>
> If truth indeed is told
> In ancient tales, or honest witness, then:
> Noble the Stone within this Chair that lies!
> Great Jacob took it for his pillow when
> That Patriarch of old
> Beheld the wondrous angels of the skies.
> Edward the First this Stone from Scotland bore
> As victor's spoils, our mightiest Hector bold;
> With puissant Mars he vied:
> Glory of England: ornament of War:
> Tamer of Scotland's pride.

40 In his rough notes for the Diary Waldstein had probably written 'of him and of his Queen': this is the magnificent Italian Renaissance tomb of Henry VII and Elizabeth of York by Torrigiano. The handsome screen around it is of English workmanship. The crowns formerly on the monarchs' heads are missing, and the attendant angels have been slightly damaged and have lost their banners, but the tomb remains otherwise as the Diary describes it. For an illustration of the tomb in its original state, see John Dart, *Westmonasterium*, I, 1723, pl. 156.

*Henry VII's Chapel in Westminster Abbey, looking past the bronze railings of the King's tomb towards the vault. Waldstein was again impressed at Windsor by such a 'profusion of beautifully worked stone pendants hanging in the English style'. (Photo Edwin Smith)*

Among other things one should see the marble throne of the Kingdom of Scotland in the royal chapel. After defeating the Scots Edward I returned triumphant in 1297 and in the Abbey of Westminster he dedicated to God the sceptre and crown of the Kings of Scotland, and also this seat upon which the Scottish Kings used to be crowned. Ever since then the throne has been kept in this royal chapel, together with a rough-hewn stone – Jacob's Stone they call it – and a tablet which hangs there with the following lines:

> *Si quid habent veri vel Chronica cana fidesque*
> *Clauditur hac cathedra nobilis ecce lapis.*
> *Ad caput eximius JACOB quondam Patriarcha*
> *Quem posuit cernens numina mira poli.*
> *Quem tulit ex Scotis spoliansque victor honoris*
> *Eduardus primus, Mars velut armipotens*
> *Scotorum domitor, noster validissimus Hector*
> *Anglorum decus, et gloria militiae.*

Among the royal chapels there is one that is royal indeed: it is a work of quite staggering architectural skill and one of the wonders of the world. Henry VII had it built with a vaulted roof of chiselled stone as a burial place for himself and his descendants forever. Further on is the very splendid tomb of his Queen done in gilded brass: a piece of magnificent workmanship. The actual figures on these tombs are of solid bronze, and gilt; on their heads are crowns which sparkle with different coloured jewels; at the head are the royal arms of England; at the feet crests, which two angels support with one hand each, their other hands holding two banners. All this is in gilded bronze.

After leaving the Abbey in Westminster we went into the neighbouring palace where the regular Courts of

41 The 'quarters of each year' are the Law terms.

42 This fountain, a conduit-head, stood in the open square outside Westminster Hall, which from the time of William Rufus to that of George IV was the scene of the Coronation Banquets.

43 This palace had formerly been Cardinal Wolsey's London residence, the property of the Archbishops of York, and had been known as York Place. Henry VIII acquired it in 1529 and renamed it 'Whitehall' (i.e. Festival Hall), the earliest known use of the new name being in 1530. (See G. S. Dugdale, *Whitehall through the Centuries*, London, 1950.)

Other visitors also found Whitehall impressive on account of its interior splendours rather than its appearance. De Maisse, French Ambassador in 1597, commented that it 'has no great appearance for a royal house'; Zinzerling wrote, 'The exterior of Whitehall Palace is not very magnificent'; and when it was destroyed by fire in 1698 Saint-Simon referred to it as 'the largest and ugliest palace in Europe'.

44 A number of the pictures mentioned in Waldstein's account were later transferred to Hampton Court. They were valued there by Cromwell's Commissioners in 1649 (Millar, *Inventories*):

| | |
|---|---|
| The blinde, Carrying the Lame at | £2: : . |
| Henry y$^e$ 8 before bullogne at | 5: : . |
| The battaile of Pavee at | 3: : . |
| Edward y$^e$ 6th lookeing through a hoole | 2: : . |

Absolute certainty about the identification of pictures is sometimes impossible. Of the doubtful pictures which Waldstein saw at Whitehall, the 'Papal battle' may be the painting of Pavia which is now in the Tower Armouries; 'Louis XII King of France' is probably the portrait attributed to Perréal in the Royal Collection; and the portrait of Richard II is probably the one in Westminster Abbey.

My most grateful thanks go to Sir Oliver Millar for the trouble he took in going through my typescript and identifying the pictures which Waldstein records.

45     The blind man bears the lame man, upon his shoulders broad,
    The cripple lends his eyes to his companion for reward.
    Each having what the other lacks, in harmony of mind
    The feet are borrowed by the lame, the eyesight by the blind.
               Mutual Assistance.

46 These pictures are still in the Royal Collection. (See Sir Oliver Millar, *Tudor, Stuart, and Early Georgian Pictures in the Collection of H.M. The Queen*, London, 1963.)

The meeting at Boulogne of Henry VIII and Francis I of France was intended as a demonstration of friendship and alliance to reinforce the effect of the famous Field of the Cloth of Gold, which had taken place twelve years before.

41 Justice are held in the quarters of each year. There is a fountain close by, and when the Kings of England are
42 crowned it flows with wine for the poor.

*Note that in all the rooms of the Queen's palace, straw has been laid to prevent noise.*

From here we then went on into the nearby palace, the royal residence known as Whitehall, i.e. the White Hall. It is truly majestic, bounded on the one side by a park which adjoins another palace which is called St James's, and on the other side by the Thames, and it is a place which fills one with wonder, not so much because of its great size as because of the magnificence of its bed chambers and living rooms which are furnished with the
43 most gorgeous splendour.

*Whitehall*

First you come to a vast hall which leads through into a very large walled garden where they keep deer and all kinds of other animals. We then went to see the rooms, every one of them furnished and arranged with perfect taste and elegance, with all sorts of statues and pictures to
44 add to their beauty. There is a bust of Attila, King of the Huns, and a circular table made of some foreign wood decorated in gold. There is a picture of a cripple
45 being carried on a blind man's shoulders with the lines:

> *Loripedem sublatum humeris fert lumine captus*
> *Et socii haec oculis munera retribuit,*
> *Quo caret alteruter concors hic praestat uterque*
> *Mutuat hic oculos, mutuat ille pedes.*
> *Mutuum auxilium*

There is the meeting of the Emperor Maximilian I and Henry VIII near Tournai and Therouanne; King Henry VIII's entry into – and his magnificent display at – Boulogne when he had made preparations to receive
46 the King of France there, done in two pictures; a portrait of Edward VI in 1546 at the age of nine – note the

*The famous anamorphosis of Edward VI, painted in 1546 and attributed to William Scrots: as it appears when viewed front-on, and viewed from an angle to 'correct' the perspective. (National Portrait Gallery, London)*

47 This trick-picture appears to have been very popular in its time and is mentioned by numerous travellers. Leopold von Wedel gives the best of the early descriptions of it: 'a picture of Edward VI, the head, face, and nose appear so long and misformed that they do not seem to represent a human being, but there is an iron bar with a plate at one end fixed to the painting: if you lengthen this bar for about three spans and look at the portrait through a little hole made in the plate, you find the ugly face changed into a well-formed one.' The bar and plate are now missing.

Shakespeare assumed that his audience were familiar with this picture or with others of the type, writing in *Richard II* (Act II, sc.ii),

> Like perspectives, which rightly gazed upon
> Show nothing but confusion; eyed awry
> Distinguish form.

48     Dance, true-born sons of England, dance you of Ireland's Isle,
    Play upon Orpheus' instrument in tunes of varied style:
    Carry the praises of our Queen over the rapid airs
    Since she, another Mary, has relieved us from our cares.

This last line, with an adulation which is fulsome beyond the bounds of good taste, compares the Virgin Queen to the Virgin Mary.

artist's ingenuity in perspective; a map of Boulogne; an extremely well-painted portrait of that Earl of Mountjoy who has just been sent to Ireland; the Papal battle in which King Francis I of France was taken prisoner by the army of Charles V in 1524; the battle of Maximilian I and Pope Julius II with Louis XII of France before Ravenna on Easter Day 1512, where 23 thousand men lost their lives; and a genealogical table of the Kings of England. There is a large looking-glass with a silk cover; a most beautifully painted picture on glass showing 36 incidents of Christ's Passion; a portrait of a woman, a goldsmith's wife, of such loveliness that she is said to have been Henry VIII's mistress. Portraits of Henry VIII King of England, Louis XII King of France, Richard II, Elizabeth Queen of Transylvania, widow of Charles XII of France, Julius Caesar, and Charles Duke of Burgundy. There are three globes; there is a ship made of gold and silver, which has its awning woven of pure silk and gold thread.

*Looking-glass*

*Glass picture of Christ's Passion*

*Ship's awning*

Another room has a picture of the battle against the Saracens in Piedmont, and the siege of Malta. There are also some very rich hangings.

A portrait here shows Queen Elizabeth when she was still young, in the dress which she wore when going to attend Parliament; there is a sundial in the form of an elephant; and an organ (in their language they call it ('an instrument') made of mother-of-pearl with the following verses inscribed on it:

*Mother-of-pearl instrument*

> *Anglica nunc plantas, plantas et Hybernia proles*
> *Orphei variis organa tange modis.*
> *Reginae laudes celeres modo ferto per aures,*
> *Subvertit nostras altra Maria lues.*

49 The Latin text could, alternatively, mean: 'with a circular piece of marble let into it'.

50 A portrait of Queen Mary of Hungary, and one of Charles V and his Queen (mentioned below), are in the Royal Collection; they are probably the pictures mentioned here.

51 Legend relates that when the Etruscan king Lars Porsena was besieging Rome (*c.* 590 BC) C. Mucius Scaevola was captured in an unsuccessful attempt to assassinate him. When brought before his intended victim he claimed that he was one of 300 Roman youths who had bound themselves by oath to take the King's life, and showed his contempt for threats of torture by thrusting his right hand into the fire and holding it there until it was consumed. Lars Porsena, impressed by the young man's valour and the threat to his own life, set him free and made peace with the city.

52 This splendid portrait by Holbein was presented to Henry VIII on New Year's Day 1539; it remained in the Royal Collection until the eighteenth century when it was transferred to the Royal Collection in Hanover. It is now in the National Gallery of Art in Washington D.C., to which I am indebted for information.

Waldstein misread his notes when writing up his Diary: the first line of the verses should end 'Haeres' not 'Heros'; and the picture shows the prince aged not twelve but less than two. The Latin verse inscription was written by Sir Richard Morison, one of Henry VIII's leading propagandists. (See Roy Strong, *Holbein and Henry VIII*, 1967.)

> Be like your father, little one,
> And to his virtues be the heir:
> The great world has not anywhere
> A thing more worthy to be done.
>
> Earth, even heaven itself, a son
> Could scarce provide, who might outvie
> So great a father's majesty.
>
> Equal his exploits! do such deeds!
> The world could never ask for more.
> But to surpass him – that exceeds
> All honoured kings who ever lived before.

53
> Pallas was keen of brain, Juno was queen of might,
> The rosy face of Venus was in beauty shining bright,
> Elizabeth then came.
> And, overwhelmed, Queen Juno took to flight;
> Pallas was silenced; Venus blushed for shame.

One of the paintings is a very lifelike representation of plums, cherries, pears, and similar kinds of fruit. There is also a rectangular table with a marble sphere on it.

In one very fine gallery or dining-hall can be seen: a mother-of-pearl bookrest; a sundial in the form of a monkey; portraits of the Prince of Orange, of Elizabeth the daughter of King Henry II of France who married King Philip of Spain, of Mary Queen of Hungary and Regent of Belgium. In addition to these are: the Duke of Savoy with his wife, his son Philibert Emmanuel, Charles V and his Queen, a painting of the story of Scaevola before Porsena King of the Etruscans, and Edward VI at the age of twelve, with the verses:

> *Parvule patrissa patriae virtutis et Heros*
> *Esto, nihil majus maximus orbis habet.*
> *Gnatum vix possunt coelum et natura dedisse*
> *Huius quem patris victus honoris honos.*
> *Aequàto tantum tanti tu facta parentis*
> *Vota hominum vix quo progrediantur habent.*
> *Vincito vicisti quot reges priscus adorat*
> *Orbis, nec te: qui vincere possit erit.*

There are maps of the Duchy of Parma, and also of Britain, both done in needlework: and a picture which shows Juno, Pallas Athene, and Venus, together with Queen Elizabeth. Beneath it are the lines:

> *Juno potens sceptris, et mentis acumine Pallas*
> *Et roseo Veneris fulget in ore decus:*
> *Adfuit ELISABETH, Juno perculsa refugit,*
> *Obstupuit Pallas, erubuitque Venus.*

In this same room see the Description of the New World on two boards with maps of the same parts of the New World alongside, printed in the reign of King Henry VII of England. There is also a diagram like an

LONDON · WHITEHALL PALACE

'The Meeting of the Emperor Maximilian and Henry VIII near Tournai and Therouanne', which Waldstein saw at the beginning of his tour of Whitehall (p. 43). The painting, by an unknown artist, shows from bottom to top the rulers' meeting in 1513, their conference, and their battle with the French. (Reproduced by gracious permission of Her Majesty the Queen)

'Juno, Pallas Athene, and Venus, together with Queen Elizabeth', by the Monogrammist HE, 1569 (see p. 47). We are meant to think of the Judgment of Paris: but it is the Queen herself who wins the prize. She is followed by her ladies-in-waiting, and in the background is perhaps the earliest painted view of Windsor Castle. (Reproduced by gracious permission of Her Majesty The Queen)

astrolabe which calculates the rising and setting of the sun. See also another board hanging here on which one can read the following story:

A certain king, seeing a revolution taking place in the kingdom, called in some Philosophers to discover the reason for this revolution. After hearing them he commanded that their opinions should, each one of them, be inscribed upon the City Gate.

The first Philosopher said:

$$\left.\begin{matrix} \text{Might} \\ \text{Day} \\ \text{Flight} \end{matrix}\right\} \text{is} \left\{\begin{matrix} \text{Right} \\ \text{Night} \\ \text{Fight} \end{matrix}\right\} \text{therefore} \left\{\begin{matrix} \text{the Realm} \\ \text{the Land} \\ \text{the Realm} \end{matrix}\right\} \text{is without} \left\{\begin{matrix} \text{Law} \\ \text{a Path} \\ \text{Honour} \end{matrix}\right.$$

The second Philospher said:

$$\left.\begin{matrix} \text{One} \\ \text{Friend} \\ \text{Evil} \end{matrix}\right\} \text{is} \left\{\begin{matrix} \text{Two} \\ \text{Foe} \\ \text{Good} \end{matrix}\right\} \text{therefore} \left\{\begin{matrix} \text{the Realm} \\ \text{the Realm} \\ \text{the Land} \end{matrix}\right\} \text{is without} \left\{\begin{matrix} \text{Truth} \\ \text{Trust} \\ \text{Reverence} \end{matrix}\right.$$

The third philosopher said:

$$\left.\begin{matrix} \text{Opinion permits licentiousness} \\ \text{The tax collector is dishonest} \\ \text{The jackdaw is an eagle} \end{matrix}\right\} \text{therefore} \left\{\begin{matrix} \text{the Realm desires anarchy} \\ \text{the Land is poverty-stricken} \\ \text{there is no wisdom in the country} \end{matrix}\right.$$

The fourth Philosopher said:

$$\left.\begin{matrix} \text{Caprice} \\ \text{Money} \\ \text{God} \end{matrix}\right\} \text{is} \left\{\begin{matrix} \text{Counsellor} \\ \text{Judge} \\ \text{Dead} \end{matrix}\right\} \text{therefore} \left\{\begin{matrix} \text{the Land is ill-governed} \\ \text{the Land is ill-guided} \\ \text{the Realm abounds in evils} \end{matrix}\right.$$

Somewhere else was written, 'There are three things which destroy the sovereignty of Rome: Hidden Hatred, Youthful Counsel, Self-Interest.'

In another place we saw a sunshade of the Queen's, made of silver and of silk, and also the Queen's couch which is woven with gold and silver thread; the same place has gorgeous mother-of-pearl caskets covered with pure silk, the Queen's chair with silken cushions, and a number of other fine cushions on the couch. The

*Silver sunshade*

54 This book appears to have been a showpiece, as it is mentioned by numerous travellers. Both the Duke of Saxe-Weimar and Eisenberg state that it was the *Dialogus Fidei* of Erasmus, so probably Waldstein is incorrect when he goes on to refer to the *Dialogus* as 'another book'.

55 This was the Shield Gallery. Pepys noted in his Diary for 22 June 1660, 'we walked a good while in the Shield Gallery', but gives no details of how it appeared in his time.

56 'The cause of strife is in the form, and not the matter.'

57 'In these and by these.'

58 'By constant dropping.'

Queen's bed-chamber has rich tapestries all around: The adjoining room is reserved for the Queen's bath: the water pours from oyster shells and different kinds of rock. In the next room there is an organ on which two persons can play duets, also a large chest completely covered in pure silk, and a clock which plays tunes by striking on bells.

The next room to this was the one where the Queen keeps her books, some of which she wrote herself. Among them there was one which she dedicated to her father as follows:

*The Queen's library*

*A treshault et trespuissant et redouble Prince Henry 8 de ce nom Roy d'Angleterre, de France, et d'Irlande, defenseur de la foy, Elisabeth sa tres humble fille, rend salut et devot obedience.*

The title-page of another book reads:

*Colloque tresfamilier entre deux personnages c'est a sçavoir Aulus et Barbatus diviser ensemble des articles de nostre foy Chrestienne, extraict des oeuvres d'Erasmi de Roterodam.*

We also saw here some prayers of Queen Catherine (the mother of Mary) which had been translated from English into Latin by Elizabeth.

On leaving here we came to a long majestic gallery where various knights have their shields displayed, painted with their devices. Among others are these:

*Causa contentionis forma non materia.*

There was a painted feather with the motto:

*Et in his et ab his.*

Another had a picture of an eye dropping tears which were watering a heart, and the motto:

*Cadendo saepe.*

59 A preferable reading occurs in John Manningham's Diary for March 1601, where he describes several of these devices: 'The scucheon argent with a hand and a pen in it, the word *Solus amor depinget.*' This would mean 'Love alone makes beautiful', i.e. 'Beauty is in the eye of the beholder'.

60 'Why do the rich complain?' Manningham writes: 'A stag having cast his head [antlers] and standing amazedly weeping over them; the word *Inermis et deformis*; under *Cur dolent habentes.*'

61       A vulture gnaws thy heart away Prometheus, but see
      Fouler by far, the vulture Love, tearing at me.

62       Spinning round for evermore, Ixion to his wheel is bound;
      I too, upon the wheel of Love am whirled incessantly around.

Ixion, with extreme ingratitude to Zeus who had purified him from former crimes, attempted to seduce Hera. He was sentenced to be bound to a fiery wheel which spins through space for ever.

63       I urge the rolling boulder up the hill,
      I, Sisyphus the wretched. Still
      Unanswered is my prayer; still the
      Relief I long for is denied to me.

Sisyphus, for betraying the secrets of Zeus and for many other crimes, was condemned by the Judges of the Dead to roll a huge boulder up a hill and topple it down on the other side. The weight of the stone is always too much for his strength and it rolls back, his prayers that he may reach the summit remaining unanswered.

64 'When one god is not forthcoming, another one brings aid.'

65 'Sorrow in servitude, toil in liberty.' Manningham describes this: 'The scucheon a grayhound coursing, with a word *In libertate labor*; and another grayhound tyed to a tree and chafinge that he cannot be loosed to followe the game he sawe: the word *In servitute dolor.*'

66 This group of nine pictures portrayed the foremost leaders of the Reformation. The majority of these men were both preachers and voluminous writers upon theological subjects. Although (with the possible exception of Zwingli) their names are now remembered only by students of theology, they were among the most influential leaders of thought in their own age. Thomas Coryat, who visited the cloisters of St Felix and St Regula at Zurich in 1608 and saw the graves of Bullinger, Peter Martyr, Gualter, and Buchmann, refers to them in his *Crudities* (1611) as men who 'by their holinesse of life, sinceritie of doctrine, and the manifold Monuments of their most learned workes, have infinitely benefited the Church of God, and purchased themselves eternitie of name till the world's end'.

Most of their names are given in classicized forms.

67 Wolfgang Müslin (i.e. 'little mouse'). I have to thank Father H. Roos, S.J., who gave me information about these reformers, for pointing out that 'patris' here refers to the Pope.

      My name is taken from the mouse; thus Fate
      Gives us sure omens, warning with this sign:
      'Huge walls the humble mice can penetrate':
      The high and haughty Papal walls I also undermine.

Another:

59    *Solus amor depingitur.*

and on another:

60    *Cur dolent habentes?*

In a different place the following verses are displayed:

61    *Cor tibi Prometheu corrodit vultur: at illo*
      *Tetrior est in me vulture, vultur Amor.*

also:

62    *Ut rota perpetuo raptans Ixiona motu*
      *Sic ego perpetuo raptus amore rotor.*

also:

63    *Sisyphus in montem volvens miser urgeo saxum*
      *Ambio nec possum quam mihi posco frui.*

also:

64    *Cum Deus unus abest, fert Deus alter opem.*

and,

65    *In servitute dolor, in libertate labor.*

In one corner there is the exceptionally large English Diamond of the Earl of Essex. A number of divines have their portraits here with their names; these are the
66    verses which go with them:

67    ***WOLFANGUS MUSCULUS***
      *Est a mure mihi nomen: sic fata dedere*
      *Omina, quae certa cum ratione monent:*
      *Maxima confodiunt contemti moenia mures,*
      *Suffodio lati moenia celsa patris.*

68 Ulrich Zwingli, who was killed at the Battle of Cappel in 1531:

> For Christ and country Zwingli spent his life,
> So, brave for Christ and country, dead he lies.
> Books show his skill, his faith Fate testifies,
> His death befits Christ's warrior in the strife.

69 Rudolf Gualter was one of the most generous of that kindly group of Swiss Protestants who offered hospitality to the English refugees from Mary's persecution when they arrived at Zurich in 1554.

> The hurrying days of forty years are flown
> Which may, I fear, conclude the life I lead.
> That which we call man's life is brief indeed,
> His care should be to live in Christ alone.

70 Simon Grynaeus (Gryner). Apollo had a famous oracle at his temple at Grynia in Asia Minor.

> If Phoebus is delighted as 'Grynaeus' to be famed
> Then rightly may Grynaeus be 'the new Apollo' named,
> And here for you his portraiture is faultlessly displayed:
> A Frisian gave the order for this painting to be made.

71 Conrad Kürschner ('tanner'), named 'Pellicanus' from the Latin *pellis*, skin. The reference in his verse is to the *Nunc dimittis*.

> I have for seventy years and more pursued my way
> Along life's path; so I, like Simeon, pray:
> 'Dismiss me now unto the shades of peace, O Lord,
> For mine eyes too have seen Christ's reign restored.'

72 Theodor Buchmann:

> Books are my great delight, books make my name,
> Such books as teach the study of God's law.
> My life has run for fifty years and four,
> And what remains shall Christ – and books too – claim.

73 Johann Hüsgen:

> Once, in God's church, a splendid light I shined,
> In Heaven's sight I held a foremost place.
> If painters could depict the heart as clearly as the face
> True doctrine would I symbolize, and piety of mind.

74 Heinrich Bullinger:

> For five and fifty years the stars glide by:
> My age of life. This little painted board
> Gives you my looks. Not looks nor life want I
> But Christ; my life and looks are in my Lord.

75 Peter Martyr (Pietro Martire) Vermigli, the foremost Italian Reformation leader. For a time he was Regius Professor of Divinity at Oxford.

> A child of Florence this: a wanderer now from place to place
> Seeking his rest as citizen among the heavenly race.
> Here is his face; his written works contain his mind and heart,
> His faith and his integrity surpass the painter's art.
> AD 1559. Aged 59.

### UDALRICUS ZVINGLIUS
Ut Christo et patriae vixit, sic fortiter uno
    Pro Christo et patria Zvinglius occubuit.
Ingenium libri, pietatem fata probarunt,
    Mors tanto Christi milite digna fuit.

### RODOLPHUS QWALTER
Octavi numero properantia tempora lustri
    Tempora cui vitae metior ipse meae.
Vita homini brevis est quae dici vita meretur,
    Sic soli CHRISTO vivere cura siet.

### SIMON GRYNAEUS
Si clari gaudet Grynaei nomine Phoebus
    Grynaeus dici fictus Apollo potest.
Quem tibi non falso pictum sub imagine vultum
    Haec Frisii iussu facta tabella refert.

### CONRADUS PELLICANUS
Bis septem lustris vixi, et qumque insuper annos
    Fatidico quare cum Simeone precor,
Nunc me dimitte in pace tenebrosa perire
    Vidimus et Christi regna redire tui.

### THEODORUS BIBLIANDER
Ex libris nomen, libri mea magna voluptas
    Qui summi tradunt iura colenda DEI.
Lustra decem vixi, nunc quatuor insuper annos
    Quod superest Christus vindicat, atque libri.

### IOANNES OECOLAMPADIUS
In Domini quondam fulsi lux splendida templo
    Cum coeli vultu conspiciendus eram,
Si veluti vultus potuissent pectora pingi
    Starem doctrinae cum pietate typus.

### HENRICUS BULLINGERUS
Undecimi iam nunc labuntur sidera lustri
    Haec aetas: formam picta tabella doret.
Nil ego vel formam vel vitae tempora specto
    Sed CHRISTUM, vita et qui mihi forma mea est.

### PETRUS MARTYR VERMILIUS
Hunc genuit Florentia: nunc peregrinus oberrat
    Quo stabilis fiat civis apud superos.
Illius effigies haec mentem scripta recondunt
    Integritas, pietas, pingier arte nequit.
        Anno 1559. Aetat 58.

76 This Banqueting Hall had been built with great speed for the coming of Alençon's ambassadors in 1581. It is described by the chronicler Holinshed (III, 1315): '... The walles of this house were closed with canuas, and painted all the outsides of the same most artificiallie with a works called rustike, much like to stone. This house had two hundred ninetie and two lights of glasse.' Holinshed then describes the ten tiers along the sides for spectators to stand on, and the decorative pendants of bay and rue, with flowers and gold spangles, and also 'hanging toseans made of hollie and iuie, with all maner of strange fruits, as pomegranats, orenges, pompions, cucumbers, grapes, carrets, with other such like, spangled with gold, and most richly hanged'.

The Banqueting Hall, which stood on the site of the present Banqueting House, was demolished in 1606. (See E. K. Chambers, *The Elizabethan Stage*, I, London, 1923, ch. I.)

77 This was the Privy Chamber, with its famous mural, painted by Hans Holbein the Younger and destroyed by the Whitehall fire of 1698. Holbein's original cartoon for the figure of Henry VIII can be seen in the National Portrait Gallery. (See Roy Strong, *Holbein and Henry VIII*, London, 1967.)

78 Henry VII, not Henry VIII, was married to Elizabeth of York.

79 If you find pleasure in seeing fair pictures of heroes
  Look then at these! None greater was ever portrayed.
Fierce is the struggle and hot the disputing; the question:
  Does father, does son – or do both – the pre-eminence win?
One ever withstood his foes and his country's destruction,
  Finally giving his people the blessing of peace;
But, born to things greater, the son drove out of his councils
  His ministers worthless, and ever supported the just.
And in truth, to this steadfastness Papal arrogance yielded
  When the sceptre of power was wielded by Henry the Eighth,
Under whose reign the true faith was restored to the nation
  And the doctrines of God began to be reverenced with awe.

80 The word used is 'muliator', which does not exist in any Latin dictionary. Waldstein may have coined the word himself from *mulier*, a woman, and the suffix -*ator* (as in *piscator*), meaning 'a catcher of', 'a user of', or 'a dealer in'. An equally probable alternative to my translation would be: 'a Londoner who was fond of women'.

81 The Battle of Muhlberg.

82 The word which I have transcribed as 'Francktrue' is largely illegible. None of the three Helmstadts in Germany claims knowledge of any famous or notorious Anthony who is buried in their town, and I should be grateful for a solution to the problem.

From here we were taken into a large and lofty banqueting hall which the Queen suddenly arranged to be put up within 20 days when she was expecting the visit of a prince of France.

In another room Henry VII and VIII and their wives are painted. With the marriage of Henry VIII to Elizabeth of York the two roses, i.e. the red and the white, are said to have grown together, for it was the King's purpose that in this marriage the struggles between the families of Lancaster and of York should come to an end. The following lines can be read here:

> *Si iuvat Heroum claras vidisse figuras,*
>    *Specta has: maiores nulla tabella tulit.*
> *Certamen magnum, lis, quaestio magna: paterne*
>    *Filius an vincat, vicit uterque quidem?*
> *Ipse suos hostes patriaeque incendia soepe*
>    *Sustulit, et pacem civibus usque dedit;*
> *Filius ad maiora quidem prognatus, ab aulis*
>    *Submovet indignos, sustituitque probos.*
> *Certe virtuti Paparum audacia cessit,*
>    *Henrico octavo sceptra gerente manu.*
> *Reddita relligio est isto regnante, DEIque*
>    *Dogmata ceperunt esse in honore suo.*

Here too they show the rock where a hermit used to live, divided into cells for him.

In another room there is a picture of a woman of Greek origin whom a London procurer brought from Greece, and who is still living. There is also a picture of the battle between Charles V and the Protestants, and a further room has a portrait of Anthony of Francktrue, whose bones are preserved at Helmstadt. There are some fine Indian beds of white and multi-coloured silk, and also a collection of small boxes and caskets made of tortoise shell.

83 These were painted and gilded heraldic beasts each carrying a vane like a small flag; they stood on wooden columns which were painted to resemble marble. They had been set up in the Whitehall garden during the reign of Henry VIII. A very rough sketch by Wyngaerde (Ashmolean Museum, Oxford) shows that the thirty-four columns were dotted about the impressively large fountain in the centre of the garden. They also appear in a painting of Henry VIII and his family (colour plate I). (See Roy Strong, *The Renaissance Garden in England*, London, 1979.)

84 Water jokes had originated in Italy. Hentzner tells us that the Whitehall fountain had a sundial nearby to attract attention, 'which, while strangers are looking at, a quantity of water forced by a wheel which a gardener turns at a distance, plentifully sprays those that are standing around'. Waldstein mentions another water joke at Theobalds on 10 July.

85 This 'other palace' was St James's Palace. If Waldstein is correct, the whale bone – which was quite a famous object – must have been moved to Whitehall not long afterwards. Henry Peacham in his rhyming hexameter introduction to Coryat's *Crudities* (1611) gives a list of the most famous sights in England and includes the whale rib:

> That horn of Windsor (of a unicorn very likely) ...
> Drake's ship at Detford, King Richard's bed-sted i'Leyster,
> The White Hall whale bones, the silver bason i' Chester

and Samuel Rowlands' *Humors Looking Glasse* (1608) also refers to it as one of London's curiosities:

> The Bosse at Billingsgate, and London stone,
> And at Whitehall the monstrous great whale's bone ...

(See G. S. Dugdale, *Whitehall through the Centuries*, London, 1950.)

86 Cecil's house was on the north side of the Strand, opposite the Savoy. William Smith, in his *A Brief Description of the famous Cittie of London* (1588), refers to it as 'a goodly house all of brick'. Sir Robert Cecil rebuilt this house (which had been his father's) soon after Waldstein's visit.

87 The famous John Whitgift, Archbishop from 1583 to 1604, Privy Councillor, and Queen Elizabeth's most trusted prelate.

88
> See how the body, frail and worn
> Is plagued by many a piercing thorn!
> Unless, to ease the heavy load, the staff of Christ is borne.

The lines refer to the arms of the See of Canterbury. The 'staff of Christ' is the archiepiscopal staff which is surmounted by a pall with four crosses fitchy. These crosses suggest the 'piercing thorn' since a 'cross fitchy' has a foot like a spike.

89 Whitgift's personal motto: 'He who suffers wins the victory.'

90
> For Nestor's years, Elizabeth, reign happy and content,
> Giver to me of many a glittering gift munificent.

91
> Together with the lilies linked, bezants of gold this promise give:
> 'He who endures his cross in pain shall after death triumphant live.'

These lines, describing Whitgift's own coat-of-arms (Argent, on a cross fleury sable, four bezants), also refer to his motto, 'Vincit qui patitur'.

A 'cross fleury' is a cross having its arms tipped with fleurs-de-lys. A bezant was originally a gold coin minted at Byzantium; the word was used by Wycliff to translate 'talentum' in the Gospels.

There is a view from the window here of a most lovely garden: it has a number of pillars with figures of animals on them; in the centre is a fountain, and water from it, squirting up through concealed pipes, soaks people standing near. Beyond the grounds of this royal residence there is another palace; it contains a rib bone from a most enormous whale which is well worth seeing.

THURSDAY, 6 JULY
Went out again in the morning for a trip in a small boat. Leaving the district of Westminster—and paying our respects to Lord Cecil en route — we went to see the Palace and Church of Lambeth, which lies beside the Thames on the opposite bank from Westminster. This Palace belongs to the Archbishop of Canterbury, and he resides there at regular intervals.

Lambeth

We first went into the former dining hall and saw there the coats-of-arms of the bishopric and the archbishopric, with the royal arms in the centre. Under the archiepiscopal arms are these lines:

> *En! leve multiplici premeretur cuspide corpus*
> *Ni baculus Christi grande levaret onus.*

and above is the motto:

> *'Vincit qui patitur.'*

Under the royal arms is:

> *Nestoreos felix regat Elisabetha per annos*
> *Quae mihi munifice candida dona dedit.*

In putting 'candida dona' he is making a pun on his own name, which in English is 'White gift'.

Under the episcopal arms:

> *Qui crucis aerumnas patitur, post fata triumphat:*
> *Lilia sic spondent fulvis coniuncta talentis.*

 *The arms of the See of Canterbury (left) and of Archbishop Whitgift.*

92 Early portraits of archbishops, which are probably those which Waldstein mentions, are at Lambeth Palace today. None of the other objects described survives.

93 The word 'Troiados' in line 4 has been miscopied: the correct reading is clearly 'Triados'.

> These, the foundations of true fame, laid down
> By the Third Edward for a Muses' shrine,
> Made the King's Hall. To them, these buildings fine
> You, Henry, added: bringing to high renown
> Our College of the Trinity divine.
>
> The church by Hervey Stanton was endowed,
> Unto the honour of St Michael vowed.

The reference is to Henry VIII's foundation of Trinity College, Cambridge, in 1546, the two colleges of King's Hall and Michaelhouse (as well as some minor hostels) being amalgamated by the King for this purpose.

Hervey de Stanton, Edward II's Chancellor of the Exchequer, had founded Michaelhouse; the allusion refers to his rebuilding of St Michael's Church as a place of worship for his own College and to its use by Trinity before the present chapel was built in Queen Mary's reign. (See A. B. Cobban, *The King's Hall, Cambridge*, and A. E. Stamp, *Michaelhouse*, Cambridge, 1924.)

*Visitors arriving, as Waldstein did, by boat at Lambeth Palace. Across the river at the left Westminster Abbey and Hall can be seen. Cecil House, where Waldstein stopped to call on Sir Robert Cecil, was on the north side of the river – above the single figure in the middle of the pier. (Drawing by Hollar. British Museum, London)*

From here we were taken upstairs to a room containing a number of portraits and paintings. Beside the door are the portraits of some of the archbishops of Canterbury. There is an unusual parchment with a list of the names of those kings, princes, and bishops who have founded, endowed with their wealth, or otherwise benefited colleges in England. First come those who have been benefactors of colleges at Cambridge or at Oxford and the following lines, in elegiacs, appear in this section:

> *Eduardus verae ponens fundamina laudis*
> *Regalem Musis extruxit Tertius aulam.*
> *Has, Henrice, domos junxisti et nobile nostrum*
> *Struxisti and summos Troiados collegium honores.*
> *Presbyteri claro decoratus nomine sancti*
> *Hervicus Stanton Michaelis condidit aedes.*

The same room contains portraits of Bullinger, Zwingli, Peter Martyr, and other preachers. The twelve tribes are also depicted. There is a splendid genealogy of all the Kings of England, and another genealogy, a historical one, which covers the whole of time and is traced down from the Beginning of the World. There are portraits of Edward the Sixth and Prince William of Orange; a very large map of Germany; a complete life of Christ in pictures; the Spanish Inquisition in Belgium; and a picture of Queen Elizabeth when she was young. On a panel is written:

These, according to the Angel, are the reasons why the Britons were driven out of their country:
'Among the prelates, idleness and evil-living; among the powerful, extortion; among the judges, greed; there was the fierce fury of desperate men; there was detestable licentiousness and shameless fashions of dress.'

94 This is an elaboration of the story told by Geoffrey of Monmouth, of how Cadwallader was warned by an angel to cease from his attempts to reconquer his kingdom, until 'the Time decreed for it was come'. Since the Tudors were of Welsh (i.e. Celtic British) origin, this story was, as Mr J. N. H. Lawrance of Magdalen College, Oxford, pointed out to me, a good piece of propaganda, probably for Henry VII.

95 The dimensions of Old St Paul's, according to the calculations of the Victorian architect E. B. Ferrey, were: height of nave, 93 feet (28.3 m); height of tower, 285 feet (87 m); length 596 feet (181.7 m).

The spire, which reached a total height of 489 feet (149 m), had been destroyed in 1561. Grenade, after telling us that during the fire the molten lead from the roof ran through the streets right down to the river, continues: 'Laquelle aiguille estoit si haute qu'on ne voit encore telle hauteur de clochier en toute l'Europe. On fait grand cas de celluy de Strasbourg, et de fait il est fort haut, mais les aiant veuz tous deux ie donne ma voix a celluy de St Paul.'

Old St Paul's, with all its contents mentioned by Waldstein, was destroyed in the Great Fire of 1666.

96 The statement is derived from Camden. It is generally accepted that Ethelbert did in fact found St Paul's. There is no archaeological proof that a temple once stood there, but it is likely that such a site should have been chosen for symbolic reasons.

97 The inscriptions on Linacre's tomb read, in translation: 'To that most renowned Physician, Thomas Linacre, this memorial was erected by John Caius M.D. August 1557.'

'Virtue survives the funeral.'

'Thomas Linacre, physician to King Henry VIII, a man of the utmost learning in the Greek and Latin tongues and also in the practice of medicine.

Many who were suffering from diseases of the liver and who had already given up all hope of recovery were by him restored to health; with an admirable and quite exceptional fluency he translated the works of Galen into the Latin tongue. Shortly before his death, at the request of his friends he edited a notable work upon an improved Latin grammar. He established in perpetuity two lectures at Oxford and one at Cambridge for the benefit of medical students. Within this City by his own efforts he caused a medical college to be founded and was himself chosen to be its first President.

Greatly hostile to fraud and deception; faithful to his friends; beloved by all sorts and conditions of men. A few years before he died he was ordained priest. He departed this life full of years and deeply regretted. 22 October, AD 1524.'

Hentzner, who also copied out this inscription, gives (with perhaps greater probability) 'aetate' for 'hepate', and Bentley translates: 'by which he restored many from a state of languishment and despair to life'.

Nevertheless, the Angel gave this answer to that same King Cadwallader: that when these sins were become as deeply rooted in the Saxons as they had been in the Britons, then would the Britons return after driving the Saxons out.

We next visited the Archbishop's library; the books all have gold or silver covers, and there we saw an ancient Bible which had its binding all of silver. There is a picture, done in feathers, of Christ in His Mother's arms; also one of a small chamaeleon. Afterwards we were taken into the garden which is quite pleasant: the most interesting object there is an English girl, done in topiary.

*The Archbishop's library*

After this visit we returned to the city and went into the principal church, St Paul's, which is famous both for its height and length. Its foundation – on the very place where a temple to Diana once stood – is attributed to Ethelbert, King of Kent. In the entrance of this church is Linacre's tomb, with the inscription:

*Thomae Linacro clariss. Medico Joh. Caius posuit Med. D. LVII. Mens: Aug.*

above this is written:

*Vivit post funera virtus*

and underneath:

*Thomas LINACRUS Henrici 8 Medicus, vir et Graece et Latine atque in re medica longe eruditissimus, multos hepate suo languentes et qui iam animum desponderant vitae restituit, Galeni opera in Latinam linguam mira et singulari facundia vertit, egregiam opus de emendata structura Latini sermonis amicorum rogatu paulo ante mortem edidit: Medicinae studiosis Oxonii publicas lectiones duas, Cantabrigiae unam in perpetuum stabilivit: in hac urbe medicorum collegium fieri sua industria curavit, eius et praesidens primus electus est. Fraudes dolosque mire perosus, fidus amicis, ordinibus omnibus juxta charus, aliquot annis antequam obiret, presbyter factus, plenus annis ex hac vita migravit, multum tum desideratus. ANNO DOMINI 1524 DIE XX Octob.*

98 Hentzner also admired Hatton's tomb, and mentions that it was ornamented with obelisks of marble and alabaster. Camden refers to it as 'that gorgeous monument right well beseeming so great a personage, which Sir William Hatton his adopted sonne consecrated to his memory in the church of St Paule in London'.
    Sir Christopher Hatton, Lord Chancellor, Privy Councillor and Knight of the Garter, had died in 1591.

99
> A gift for worms I lie below,
> And in this way I try to show
> That, just as I am buried, so
> The glory of this world shall go.

The doggerel of my translation reflects something of the absurd jingle of the original.

100 This was the tomb of John of Gaunt (Waldstein should have written 'Duke' instead of 'Earl'). Of the seven tombs in St Paul's which Grenade considered to be of special interest, he named this first.

101 The eastern part of the vast crypt under Old St Paul's was the separate parish church of St Faith's (removed there in the thirteenth century when the original church was demolished to make way for eastward enlargement of St Paul's). It is mentioned in Thomas Dekker's delightful play *The Shoemaker's Holiday*, of 1600 (Act IV, sc.ii):

> 'Where must Master Hammon be married?'
> 'At St Faith's church under Paul's.'

Waldstein implies (and perhaps thought) that the whole crypt was St Faith's.

102 Sermons, attended by the Lord Mayor and other notables, were preached outside the Cathedral at St Paul's Cross. The Cross stood on the north-east side and not 'in front of the church'.

103 The Tower did then have 'triple walls'. The inner bailey was demolished in the late seventeenth century.

104 By the early seventeenth century a whole mass of housing had developed within the Tower walls. Much of it was cleared away during the eighteenth and nineteenth centuries.

105 Hentzner was also impressed by the Tower Armoury, and wrote: 'But who can relate all that is to be seen here?' The Tower still contains one of the finest collections of arms and armour in the world.

106 The National Maritime Museum at Greenwich informed me that both chain-shot and bar-shot existed at this time. Both can be seen at the Tower. Bar-shot consists of two iron balls connected by a short iron bar: when fired from an unrifled barrel the missile would be sure to spin, and would have a much better chance of cutting ropes and spars than a single shot.
    Chain-shot consists of iron balls linked by a chain, or an iron ball cut into three, the pieces being loosely chained. They were fitted together before being loaded, but when fired the pieces would fly apart as far as the chains allowed, and – like bar-shot – would do far more damage to rigging than a simple cannon ball.

The most splendid and beautiful monument in the church is undoubtedly Chancellor Hatton's, made of black and white marble and ornamented with gold.

On one of the tombstones in the floor you can find these verses:

> *Vermibus hic donor, et sic ostendere conor*
> *Hic veluti ponor, sic erit orbis honor.*

The church contains a chapel which was originally intended for storing church vestments; here the Earl of Lancaster lies buried.

Down below there is a crypt or another church underground which is just as large in area as the one above it. In front of the church there is an open space where they hold open air services which the Mayor of the City himself attends. The services last for nearly 3 hours.

## Friday, 7 July

Visited the castle by the Thames: it is usually called the Tower of London. It is defended with several moats, encircled by triple walls, and inside it is so full of houses that it gives visitors the impression of a town. A large open space in front of the Tower contains four scaffolds, and here a number of dukes, earls, and others have been executed for treason.

*The Tower of London*

The Armoury in the Tower is particularly interesting, with a fine collection of cannon, pikes, shields, missiles, arrows, cross-bows, javelins, and other weapons.

First of all, downstairs, we were shown some twenty siege-guns mounted on gun-carriages, and here we saw those iron devices which they fire from naval guns to destroy ships' rigging, for these English guns are most commonly used in battles at sea. Nearby we were shown

107 The 'morning-star' was a generously spiked steel ball or cylinder mounted on a wooden shaft.

108 The word 'arquebus' is derived from the German *Hakenbüchse*, meaning a hook-gun. Early portable guns were heavy and had a powerful recoil, so they were provided with a hook in order that their weight could be taken by some convenient battlement or rampart. During the sixteenth century the French form of the word, 'arquebuse', had come into general use for all portable firearms except for the pistol.

109 The 'gun which fires seven times' was destroyed in the Tower fire of 1841.

110 This three-barrelled gun is still in the Tower. It bears the name of Henry VIII and has his Tudor Rose between two putti. It was badly damaged in the 1841 fire. I could not actually get my fist inside the muzzle, but the calibre is 2.1 inches and it would certainly take a sizeable egg.

111 The spears, still at the Tower, bear a Tudor rose in punched decoration, and were carried by Henry VIII's Guard. They no longer have silk and gold tassels.

112 This weird weapon, which is still exhibited at the Tower, is a special version of the type euphemistically called a 'holy water sprinkler'; it was also known as 'Henry VIII's walking-stick'. It is recorded in two early inventories: 1547 ('Holly water sprincles wt thre gonnes in the Topp, oone'), and 1676 ('King Henry ye 8ths walking staff').

113 These shields were made for Henry VIII by Giovanbattista da Ravenna. There are two types: one with the gun placed above the centre of the shield, the other with the gun mounted in the shield's central boss. They can still be seen in the Tower Armoury.

114 'Almost covered with rust'; Hentzner suggests this with more tact, writing: 'Eight or nine men employed by the year are scarce sufficient to keep all the arms bright.'

a place which had 16 cases or containers full of great
107  iron pikes, with six morning-stars on either side, and in
another place was a store filled with very long wooden
lances tipped with buttons. There were arrows which
can be loaded into guns, and – just the reverse – bows
which can shoot leaden bullets. Into the arquebus,
between the powder and the arrows, they put some
leathery substance the length of a man's finger, for setting
108  ships on fire. Further on we saw barbed arrows which at
the same time pierce the flesh and burn from the pitch
smeared on them, and because of this – as with Turkish
arrows – they cannot be pulled out except by cutting the
whole body open.

Downstairs they showed us mortar bombs full of
gunpowder, and here we saw a gun which fires seven
times at one loading: it has seven apertures above from
which the shot is fired, and seven below where the
109  powder is ignited. We noticed another gun of the same
type with three mouths, each of them as wide as an egg
110  or a clenched fist.

We then visited another armoury full of spears
111  decorated with silk and gold, belonging to the Royal
f.145  Guard. We saw weapons which can be used by turns as
guns or hammers, and one which is at the same time a
112  gun with 3 barrels, a pike, and a long walking-stick. In
addition there were shields from which bullets can be
113  fired, and pikes with which one can give both a cutting
and a thrusting blow. Next we came to a room
containing some iron breastplates almost covered with
114  rust; the most astonishing things here were some cuirasses
of enormous size.

# THE TOWER OF LONDON

The Tower, from a panorama by Anthonis van den Wyngaerde, c. 1550. A river entry leads in through Traitors' Gate; on the quay are cannon and cranes. In the centre is the White Tower, 'Built, so they say, by Julius Caesar'. Tower Hill lies outside the picture to the left. (From a facsimile of the drawing in the Ashmolean Museum, Oxford)

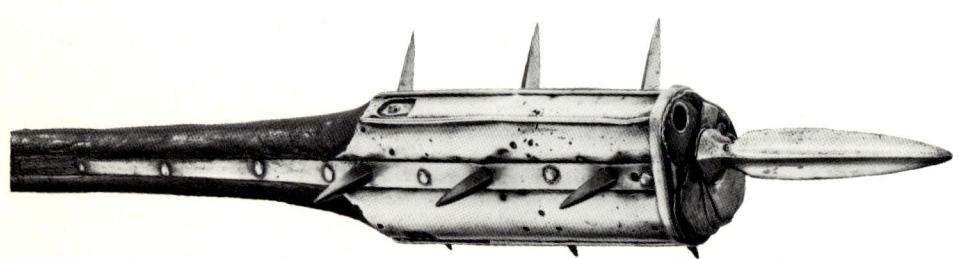

The head of 'King Henry VIII's Walking-stick', a weapon 'which is at the same time a gun with 3 barrels, a pike, and a long walking-stick'. (Armouries, H. M. Tower of London)

*(above)* One of the gun-shields made for Henry VIII by Giovanbattista da Ravenna. The gun-barrel is placed in the centre, and the defender looks out through a grill above it. *(Armouries, H. M. Tower of London)*

*(right)* The gun 'with three mouths, each of them as wide as an egg or a clenched fist': a brass gun cast for Henry VIII by Peter Baude about 1540, with engraved decoration and the Tudor rose. *(Armouries, H. M. Tower of London)*

115 The keep or White Tower, built by William the Conqueror, was known as Caesar's Tower. The '16 cannon' were Spanish guns captured by Essex at Cadiz in the famous raid. Several diarists mention them, the Duke of Stettin-Pomerania's Diary stating that there were 17 of them. The guns are just visible in Haiward and Gascoyne's *A true and exact Draught of the Tower Liberties, survey'd in the year 1597*.

116 The room still exists; it is hardly a 'turret', but since it was pointed out from the roof of the White Tower Waldstein may have made a mistake in its exact location. Queen Elizabeth had been kept there under close surveillance for two months in 1554.

117 The 'Earl of Northumberland' was Henry Percy, the 8th Earl. His family suffered considerably under the Tudors, his father being executed by Henry VIII for having played a leading part in the 'Pilgrimage of Grace', his brother being executed for his part in the Northern Rebellion, and he himself suffering several terms of imprisonment for his attempts to secure the escape of Mary Queen of Scots. During his third imprisonment for an attempt to do this and also to obtain toleration for the Catholics, in June 1585, he was found dead in his cell, shot through the heart. Naturally most Catholics (and probably some others) believed that he had been murdered, but a jury returned a verdict of suicide and this verdict was subsequently confirmed by a Star Chamber inquiry.

118 What Waldstein writes here concerning Desmond's escape and the reason for his imprisonment is inaccurate. At about the age of fourteen he had been taken to the Tower after his father had renounced allegiance to the Queen. He remained there for the following sixteen years, but not long after Waldstein's visit he was taken back to Ireland. He was intended to be a rival Earl of Desmond to his Roman Catholic cousin James.

119 The original Great Hall, built by Henry III c. 1236, which had fallen into disuse when the Tower ceased to be a residential palace. Anne Boleyn had stood her trial here. In Haiward and Gascoyne's plan the room is depicted as a bare space open to the sky with the description: 'The Hall, Decay'd'.

120 This seems an enormous number, but Hentzner estimated it as 'above a hundred'.

121 The Windischgraetz brothers were close friends of Waldstein's; they first appear in the Diary in 1597 as his fellow-students at Strasbourg, and they had been with him during part of his stay in France. Their branch of the family came, Prince Windischgraetz informed me, from Regensburg in Germany; they had migrated there from Austria early in the sixteenth century after having lost their property on their conversion to the Lutheran faith. The Regensburg branch of the family is now extinct.

Then we climbed a tower with a leaden roof – built, so they say, by Julius Caesar – where there are 16 cannon which are trained upon the City. From here they pointed out the place, an insignificant but wide turret, where Queen Elizabeth was kept prisoner: only twice was she allowed to go into the garden alongside. Also of interest is the cell where the Earl of Northumberland committed suicide. What is more, we saw Earl Desmond, of Ireland, for 19 years a prisoner, and this because when still a boy he had said that he would be revenged for his father's death. Just recently however, while we were still in England, we heard that he had escaped.

After that we saw an ancient dining-hall, almost falling to pieces with age: this too they attribute to Julius Caesar; in addition to all this we saw sixty tapestries, very richly and splendidly worked with gold thread. There was a coffer containing cushions and other bed furnishings embroidered with immensely valuable pearls and precious stones, and numerous chairs which had their cushions woven in mixed silk and gold thread. Particularly impressive was an extremely rich curtain embroidered with huge pearls; and there was also another curtain, very large, of cloth-of-gold.

In the evening, when nearly everyone had already gone to bed, the Windischgraetzes arrived, and Stadler with them.

SATURDAY, 8 JULY
Hired horses for our trip through England. On the orders of Lord Cecil, Chief Secretary of the English Realm (to whom we had been given letters of

122 Stephen Lesieur, formerly secretary to the French ambassador, had been taken into the public service by Cecil a few years previously. He was employed in various diplomatic duties under Elizabeth and also under James I, who granted him a pension and knighted him. He accompanied Waldstein back to France on affairs of State.

123 Henry VII had demolished Humphrey, Duke of Gloucester's Palace of Bella Court and had built his own Tudor Palace of 'Placentia' ('Pleasaunce') on its site. It had three courtyards and was built of brick and stone in the general style of Hampton Court. It was the birthplace of Henry VIII and was known to be his favourite place. No fragments of this Tudor building now remain.

124 In 1592 Jacob Rathgeb had the same very pleasant impression of the good manners of the English aristocracy: 'even great English lords made way for us and put us forward that we might better see the Queen – a thing indeed which rarely occurs to the attendants of foreign ambassadors'.

125 This was the normal costume of the Maids of Honour. The Sidney Family Papers (II, 170) contain a letter to Sir Robert Sidney from Rowland Whyte (24 February 1599) describing an Audience: 'and soe he entred the Presence Chamber, full of great Ladies, and the faire Maides, attired all in White, excellently brave'. (For the Sidney Papers see note 5.)

View of Greenwich Palace from One Tree Hill, painted about 1600 by an unknown artist. In the far distance is the City of London. (National Maritime Museum, Greenwich)

introduction by Lord Neville, the English Ambassador at Boulogne), Stephen Lesieur was sent to us so that he could present me to the Queen, but although he enquired for me – twice – at our lodging he got no proper reply from the staff, so it was all in vain.

## Sunday, 9 July

In the morning we took a small boat to Greenwich Palace, 4 miles from London, a royal residence and the birthplace of the Queen. Our great eagerness to see the Queen kept us from leaving, and here Monsieur Lesieur met us (he had been sent to us for this very reason at the Queen's command by Mr Secretary Cecil) and at 10 o'clock he took us inside the Palace and into the room they call the Presence Chamber where a crowd of famous people and noblemen was gathered.

Then, dressed in white and silver, the Maids of Honour (their beauty and shapeliness had no difficulty in diverting the eyes and minds of some of the spectators) made ready for the entrance of the Queen and of those who were to escort her to the chapel. A procession came first, led by the Chancellor carrying a gold-embroidered purse bearing the royal insignia, and a Knight of the Garter holding a sword before him, and Secretary Cecil following; then she herself, glittering with the glory of majesty and adorned with jewellery and precious gems, entered into the view of the whole assembly and stretched her arms out wide as if to embrace everybody present. At her entry everyone knelt.

She had already been told of my arrival and asked at once where I was and what language I spoke. Quite soon she identified me, and speaking in English said

*Greenwich*

*The courtesy of the English to foreigners is worth noting, for when we were in the Queen's hall, really distinguished persons willingly gave up their places to us.*

NB.

126 Unfortunately Waldstein does not give the actual words of the Queen's greeting. What he writes is: 'dicens Anglice: Adventus tuus mihi est gratus'. Dr A. L. Rowse kindly informed me that on such an occasion the Queen would not have used the royal 'we'.

127 The phrase which the Queen teased him by pretending to misunderstand is 'praesentiam longe superare famam' (in his speech of farewell). The Latin *could* be taken ambiguously, and would mean 'that your fame far surpasses your real self', instead of – as of course he actually meant – that she herself far surpassed all reports of her.

128 'Whoever speaks to her, it is kneeling; now and then she raises someone with her hand.' (Hentzner)

129 Waldstein's uncle, Hynek Brtnický z Valdštejna, had visited England on a diplomatic mission.

126 graciously: 'I welcome you.' She heard me patiently to the end of what was certainly rather a long speech, and then, very gracious, deigned to give me a most kind reply. And when, among other things, I said that in reality she far surpassed the reports about her, then she interrupted me, putting the wrong meaning on my words, and said: *'This shall be your lordship's punishment – you have perhaps heard more than you are going to see: pay*
127 *somewhat less attention to rumour.'*

Actually, before I could address the Queen, to declare how great her goodness was, she first stretched out her hand for me to kiss, and immediately afterwards she
128 raised me to my feet.

## My Speech of Greeting

Most Serene and Illustrious Queen, and Most Gracious Sovereign Lady:

f.147  Ever since I left my schooldays behind me and, with the encouragement and advice of my family, began travelling in foreign lands, I have hoped and prayed for nothing so much as that I too, as my ancestors and
129 kinsmen have done before me, might one day set foot in this glorious Kingdom of England, and that at the same time I might come face to face into the presence of Your Majesty which fills the whole world with glory and indeed with wonder also – and be allowed to offer you my service and most humble duty.

I am therefore exceedingly happy that – by the grace of Almighty God and Your Majesty's great favour – I

*Speech of greeting to the Queen*

*A unique depiction of Queen Elizabeth receiving ambassadors – envoys from the Protestant Netherlands – who kneel before her. The setting of this still rather mysterious painting by a visiting German must be the Audience Chamber, and the time about 1586. (Staatliche Kunstsammlungen, Kassel)*

have today obtained my desire; and I count this as the greatest part of my good fortune: that I have been admitted into Your Majesty's presence and have been received with so much kindness. With no less humble submission I pray that Your Majesty may write my name among the number of your most faithful and dutiful servants, and not think me unworthy to feel the fair wind of your favour.

I hope and pray that Almighty God will strengthen your throne and continue to grant you a long life and vigorous old age, so that this kingdom, which with Your Majesty sitting at the helm has been peaceful and secure while other parts of the world have been troubled by the fearful storms of war, may continue to experience peace and prosperity; and most especially I pray that the Church, of which Your Majesty is the most gracious guardian, may enjoy halcyon tranquillity for many years.

And may your subjects, whose well-being is one with
Your Majesty's, ever prosper in body, soul,
and in fortune, with an abundance
of all blessings.


*My Speech of Farewell*


I am overwhelmed with delight, Most Illustrious Queen and my Most Gracious Sovereign Lady, in having achieved the greatest object of my journey. It is known far and wide, indeed it is reported everywhere, that the exceeding graciousness and the wisdom of Your Majesty

130 The reference is to Plato (*Laws*, IV): 'When the supreme power is united with the greatest wisdom and temperance, then do the best laws and the best constitution come into being, and in no other way.'

131 For the quotation from the Queen of Sheba's speech to Solomon (I Kings 10: 8) I have used the words of the 'Bishops' Bible' of 1572 which was then the standard translation. The wording differs only very slightly from that of the Authorized Version.

are equally worthy of admiration: now I too have had experience of this for myself, and have discovered that your real self far surpasses your fame. Your Majesty has indeed confirmed the philosopher's saying, that 'the happiest country, and that which is most free from ills, is the one where, by some divine providence, a mighty ruling power is united with wisdom and justice'. To you, therefore, a Queen resplendent with so much Majesty, I can truly say with that other Queen: 'Happy are these thy servants which stand continually before thee and that hear thy wisdom.'

    I can never fully express how much it means to me that Your Majesty has stooped so low from the height of your royal dignity as to treat me with a kindness of which I know myself to be unworthy, and for this cause I acknowledge myself and those who are mine as forever indebted to and under an obligation to Your Majesty. And although my efforts can no more enhance your renown than my lamps can light up the sun, yet I shall not cease from devoting myself to proclaiming, wheresoever I find myself, the extreme goodness of Your Majesty to me, so that the whole world may know the adoration with which I look up to, revere, and worship Your Majesty, as some goddess come down from the skies.

    In conclusion once again I humbly pray that I may be added to the roll of Your Majesty's dutiful servants. And I pray Almighty God to prolong Your Majesty's life for many years,
and I also pray for the Church and People of England
that He may long preserve them in prosperity
and happiness.

132 These letters were signed by Sir Robert Cecil, as appears in the letter from Robert Soame quoted in note 152.

133 The Yeomen Warders in their summer liveries. Chambers describes these liveries as: 'gorgeous and costly, of scarlet cloth, with spangles and embroidery of Venice gold taking the shape of a rose and crown and the letters E.R.' (*The Elizabethan Stage*, 1, London, 1923, p. 52).

134 This reference to the nobleman and the cloaks, which I have placed between dashes, is an interpolation by Waldstein in very small writing between the lines. He did not correct the verbs which follow into the plural, however, and since it was clearly the 'graceful and beautifully dressed girl' who was in his mind rather than the nobleman, I have so translated.

135 This kneeling at the entrance and in the centre of the room was a sign of respect to the chair of state. When the Duke of Bracciano, Don Virginio Orsini (Shakespeare's Orsino?) wrote to his 'Signora Consorte amatissima' on 18 January 1600 describing Twelfth Night festivities at Whitehall, where he had been a highly honoured guest, he narrates: 'Meanwhile came the viands of her Majesty, borne by knights, and the Sewer was of the great Order [the Garter]. These did the same honour to her Majesty's chair of state as they would have done had she been present.' (From Leslie Hotson, *The First Night of Twelfth Night*, London, 1954.)

136 Theobalds (which was always pronounced 'Tibbalds') was one of the sights of the kingdom: the diary of the Duke of Württemberg describes it as: 'the magnificent palace Theobalds, belonging to the Lord High Treasurer of England, which is reckoned one of the most beautiful houses in England, as indeed it is'.

The mansion had been built by William Cecil in 1560. John Nichols' *Progresses . . . of Queen Elizabeth* (London, 1788–1821) reports that the Queen was twelve times at Theobalds, and that each visit cost Cecil two or three thousand pounds. James I stopped there on his way to London upon his accession to the throne, and according to Stow he received 'entertainment such and so costly as can hardly be expressed'. At Theobalds James entertained his brother-in-law King Christian IV of Denmark for four days, and took such a liking to the place that in the following year (1607) he persuaded Cecil to exchange it for Hatfield.

Despite the report of Cromwell's Commissioners in 1650 that this splendid palace was 'an excellent building, in very good repair, by no means fit to be demolished' (Millar, *Inventories*) almost all the building was pulled down under the Commonwealth, the proceeds from the sale of the materials being distributed among the army.

Theobalds was very large: it had two great courts, and also a dial court, a buttery court, and a dove-house court. The main court was 110 feet (33.5 m) square; the fountain court 86 feet (26.2 m) square, with a cloistered walk along the east side. There was a Presence Chamber, and the survey refers to its roof of beams and 'gilded pendants hanginge downe, setting forth the roome with greate splendor: as alsoe with verie large windowes, and several coates of armes sett in the same'. The Green Gallery, which was 109 feet long by 12 wide (33.2 by 3.6 m), was 'excellently well painted round with the several shires in England, and the armes of the noblemen and gentlemen in the same'. (See D. Lysons, *Environs of London*, London, 1792–96, IV.)

Those fragments of Theobalds which survived Cromwell's regime were almost completely demolished in the last half of the eighteenth century. Still standing are a few feet of wall with a blocked-up window, and a small portion of the entrance porch to the south range of the palace.

After I had finished my speech, which was in Latin, the Queen replied to me and began: 'I understand that your lordship has asked for letters — which you shall have.' She promised me then and there that all the doors of her kingdom should be open to me, and gave commands for letters of introduction to be written to the Governors of the most important castles and palaces, and to the Vice-Chancellors of the universities.

Then she went into the chapel for prayers, and remained there for a quarter of an hour or twenty minutes before returning to the room for a meal. We saw the food being brought into the Presence Chamber by a large number of rather elderly servants wearing red liveries with the Queen's badge. Next, a graceful and beautifully dressed girl — together with a nobleman, both of them wearing cloaks hanging from the shoulders — appeared, and, first in the doorway, then in the middle of the room, and finally at the place where the meal had been laid, she went down on her knees and — as if saying her prayers — examined every dish: from each one which they had brought in she handed over something to be tasted.

After this visit we went with M. Lesieur to an inn where we lunched; in the evening we took a small boat back to London.

MONDAY, 10 JULY
Started out from London at about 8 a.m. to see Cambridge University. First we came to the mansion of Theobalds. This is 12 miles from London and was built by Treasurer William Cecil; it is now the property of his son Robert Cecil, Secretary to the Queen. Both the architecture and the furnishings of this great house are

*Theobalds, the mansion of the Secretary of England*

Sir Robert Cecil, owner of Theobalds and later builder of Hatfield, who received Waldstein in London, secured his audience with the Queen, and introduced him to the Vice-Chancellor of Cambridge. (Portrait by Jan de Critz the Elder; this version dates from 1602. National Portrait Gallery, London)

137 Rathgeb describes them in more detail: 'On each side of the hall are six trees, having the natural bark so artfully joined, with birds' nests and leaves as well as fruit upon them, all managed in such a manner that you could not distinguish between the natural and these artificial trees.'

magnificent, and in addition it is notable for the number of its turrets and for its unrivalled fireplaces.

Inside the gate house, between two pillars on the wall, there is a container which is elaborately constructed to look like a bunch of grapes: it has been made with such ingenuity that when the Queen is present they draw white wine from one part of it and red wine from another. The same room has a picture showing Brazilians in their native dress.

There is a fountain in the centre of the garden: the water spouts out from a number of concealed pipes and sprays unwary passers-by. Quite a large obelisk of alabaster surmounted by a figure of Christ stands in the garden; nearby is an alabaster sundial, and the royal arms of England are displayed here surrounded by the Garter in gold. On the way up to the house there is a fountain: a little ship of the type they use in the Netherlands is floating on the water, complete with cannons, flags, and sails.

In the first room there is an overhanging rock or crag (here they call it a 'grotto') made of different kinds of semi-transparent stone, and roofed over with pieces of coral, crystal, and all kinds of metallic ore. It is thatched with green grass, and inside can be seen a man and a woman dressed like wild men of the woods, and a number of animals creeping through the bushes. A bronze centaur stands at the base of it. A number of columns by the windows support the mighty structure of the room: these columns are covered with the bark of trees, so that they do in fact look exactly like oaks and pines. In this same room there is an exceedingly fine alabaster fireplace, and also another in black and white marble.

138    The busts were of the same Emperors who appeared in the coloured portraits, i.e. the first twelve Caesars whose biographies were written by Suetonius.

139    Many of the pictures remained at Theobalds after the 1607 exchange of the mansion for the Palace of Hatfield. In 1640 Theobalds was visited by the Signor de Mandelslo who lists several portraits which Waldstein had seen there at the beginning of the century: 'Dans une autre galerie, se voyent les portraits de Jules Cesar & d'Auguste, Empereurs Romains: de Dom Jean d'Autriche, fils naturel de Charles quint, qui gagna la bataile de Lepante contre les Turcs, & qui fut Governeur des Pays Bas, ou il mourut; de Louis Prince de Condé: d'Alexandre Duc de Parme; des Comtes d'Egmont et de Horn, qui furent executez a Bruxelles l'an 1568 par les ordres du Duc d'Albe, contre le droit des gens. Au dessus étoient peintes les principales Villes du monde.' (Hatfield House Papers, also *Les Voyages du Sieur Albert de Mandelslo*, Leiden, 1719.)

At Hatfield House today there are portraits of Richard III, and of Henry V, VI, and VII, which are known to have been there since 1612. They are almost certainly those which Waldstein saw at Theobalds.

140              Offer to Mary roses, in purity of heart
              And she will give you blessed fruit from Heaven.

Another room has coloured portraits of the Roman Emperors from Julius Caesar to Domitian, busts of the 12 Caesars sculpted in some special material, a terrestrial globe which is 12 spans in circumference, pictures of some of the Knights-Commander of the Golden Fleece, and also of the following Kings: Richard III, Henry IV, Edward IV, Henry V, VI, VII. On the opposite wall are portraits of Don John of Austria, the Duke of Parma, Count d'Egmont, the Admiral of France, the Prince de Condé, and the Duke of Saxony; in addition there are views of a number of important cities, and a very handsome table of black marble. A further gallery downstairs shows portraits of the Cecil family, with an account of the notable acts of each under different reigns.

In a different part of the house there is a room containing valuable hangings and various other bed-furnishings: one bed has its coverlet woven of gold, another is made of ostrich feathers, and there are hangings which are made – with wonderful skill – out of multi-coloured straw. There is a draughts board with all the pieces made of gold and silver, an oil-lamp made of gold, and a painting on the wall of Queen Elizabeth's coronation. There is another picture with the inscription:

> *Vos Mariae praebete rosas, de cordeque puro*
> *Illa ex Empyreo poma beata dabit.*

Upon the roof of the house there is a splendid gallery from which you can see the Tower of London. An aqueduct brings water right up here to the top of the building, and from here to all the rest of the mansion; there is also an Astronomers' Walk on the roof-top.

One of the rooms contains a picture of Edward VI with the words:

141 'Edward VI King of England and Defender of the Faith, on Earth the Head, next under Our Saviour Christ, of the Church of England and of Ireland'.

142 This mural of the counties and county families of England impressed several diarists. The best description apart from Waldstein's own is that of Signor de Mandelslo (see note 139): 'On y voit dans une grande galerie toutes les provinces du royaume avec leurs villes, chateaux, villages, forets, rivieres, montagnes, et valées, peintes a l'huile, et en chaque province un arbre ayant ses branches chargées des armes des seigneurs et des gentilshommes du lieu.'

Cambridge, seen across open fields from the west. The view is dominated by King's College Chapel, 'lovely and kingly indeed'. Other buildings shown, from left to right, are Trinity Church (11), Caius (12), St Andrew's (13), Great St Mary's (14), St Edward's (15), Clare Hall (17), St Catharine's Hall (18) and Queen's (19). (Detail from David Loggan's 'Cantabrigia Illustrata', 1680s)

*Eduardus VI rex Angliae, et fidei defensor in terra Ecclesiae Anglicae et Hybernicae, immediate sub Christo servatore nostro caput.*

Another room displays the coats-of-arms of the earls and barons of England: all round the walls are trees painted in green, one tree for every county in England, and from their boughs hang the arms of those earls, barons, and nobles who live in that particular county. The specialities of any county are included, so if one of them is outstandingly rich in flocks and herds it has them painted here also, and if some fruit or other is particularly abundant, then you find it recorded in the same way.

In the garden you see lilies and other flowers growing among the shrubs: the garden also contains some alabaster busts of the Caesars. An outstanding feature is a delightful and most beautifully made ornamental pool (at present dry, but previously supplied with water from 2 miles away): it is approached by 24 steps leading up to it. The water was brought up to this height by lead pipes and it flowed into the pool through the mouths of two serpents. In two of the corners of this pool you can see two wooden water-mills built on a rock, just as if they were on the shores of a river. The roof itself is painted in tempera with appropriate episodes from history, and is very finely vaulted. A space beside the pool houses white marble statues of the 12 Roman Emperors.

After leaving this mansion we went a further 9 miles through a number of villages until we came to Ware, a town in Essex, and here we stopped for a light meal. Setting out at about three o'clock from here we covered 24 miles at our best speed and finally reached the town of *Cantabrigia*, commonly called Cambridge, just as night was beginning to fall.

Cambridge

143 The description of Cambridge has been taken – though not verbatim – from Camden's *Britannia*.

144 Mr J. N. H. Lawrance, Fellow of Magdalen, reviewing my translation, commented: 'as an Oxford man I must point out that "alter" normally means the *second* of two, not merely *one* of two!' He is of course correct, but I support my version with Holland's rendering (1610) of this same passage of the *Britannia* which Waldstein used: 'This City which being the other University of England, the other eye, the other strong-staie as it were thereof, and a most famous mart & store-house of good literature and Godlinesse, standeth upon the river Cam.'

145 The story that the University was founded by Cantaber and subsequently refounded by Sigebert is as totally unhistorical as the similar – but even more exaggerated – claim that Oxford was founded in the days of the prophet Samuel. Each University wished to claim seniority, so that, as the historian Maitland remarked. 'The oldest of all inter-university contests was a lying match.'

The story of Cantaber (the earliest known reference to it is in Bishop Fisher's oration to Henry VII on the occasion of his visit to Cambridge in 1506) appears to have been accepted for many years and it is retold (with circumstantial details of the marriage of Cantaber to the daughter of King Gurguntius, and of his providing the new University with philosophers hired from Athens) in the Cambridge University Calendar for 1787.

King Sigebert's reputation outlasted even Cantaber's: he did not slip out of the official list of royal benefactors until the present century.

146 Simon Bibye (Bibeus) had published a list of colleges with their dates and founders; Camden, John Caius (in *De antiquitate Cantabrigiensis Academiae*, 1574), and the *Skeletos Cantabrigiae* manuscript (in Caius College Library) provide others. Waldstein follows none of these precisely, and I have not discovered his source either for this list or for the one which he later gives of the Oxford colleges. It is clear, however, that he used the same source as Hentzner did.

These lists of colleges differ in details from one another, possibly because of the difficulty of deciding exactly *when* a college is founded: when it is first endowed? when it receives its charter? or when its Fellows and students are first incorporated?

Waldstein's list gives the names of the founders correctly except for the founder of Trinity Hall, who was not John Crawden but William Bateman, Bishop of Norwich. John de Crawden had built a hostel for student-monks from Ely and this hostel was purchased by Bateman for Trinity Hall.

143 Cambridge is famous for its university and colleges rather than for the size of its buildings. It is one of
144 England's two universities — one of two eyes as it were — and is known far and wide as a storehouse of religious learning and humane studies. It has sixteen extremely beautiful colleges (each with its own library, hall, and cloisters); they are real shrines of the Muses, large numbers of exceedingly learned men are maintained there, and indeed knowledge of the Arts and skill in languages flourish there so greatly that the colleges are considered, and with perfect justice, to be the very fountains of learning, religion, and liberal education, gently watering the gardens of Church and State with their health-giving streams.

The town's latitude is 52′, its longitude 23′.

The University is said to have been first established in 375 BC by the Spaniard Cantaber, and to have been
145 refounded in AD 630 by Sigebert, King of East Anglia.
146 The first college (Peterhouse) was founded and endowed in 1280 by Hugh Balsham, Bishop of Ely.

Clare Hall in 1326 by Richard Badew, with the aid of Elizabeth Clare, Countess of Ulster.

Pembroke Hall in 1343 by Mary de St Pol, Countess of Pembroke.

Corpus Christi College in 1344 by the Society of Brothers of Corpus Christi.

Trinity Hall in 1354 by John Crawden.

The College of Gonville and Caius by Edmund Gonville in 1348, and by John, a Doctor of Medicine of our own times.

King's College in 1441 by Henry VI, King of England: he added the chapel which rightly claims its

There are sixteen Cambridge colleges.

1. Peterhouse

2. Clare

3. Pembroke

4. Corpus Christi

5. Trinity Hall

6. Gonville and Caius

7. King's

'The new college – or palace rather – of Sidney'. Loggan's view shows Hall Court (now much altered), which had just been completed in Waldstein's time. The 'particularly splendid hall' lies at the back of the court on the left, labelled C. (Detail from 'Cantabrigia Illustrata', 1680s)

place as one of the loveliest buildings in the world.

Queens' College in 1448 by Margaret of Anjou, his wife.

Jesus College is of the same date, founded by John Alcock, Bishop of Ely.

St Catharine's Hall in 1459 by Robert Woodlark.

Christ's College and John's College in about 1506 by Margaret Richmond, the mother of King Henry VII.

Magdalene College by Thomas Audley the English Chancellor; Sir Christopher Wray the Lord Chief Justice of England endowed the College both with buildings and with property.

Trinity College in 1546 by Henry VIII.

Emmanuel College was founded recently by Sir Walter Mildmay, Knight of the Garter and Her Majesty's Privy Councillor.

In addition to these there is the new college – or palace rather – of Sidney.

The colleges have very large revenues so that the income of each may amount to seven thousand pounds or thereabouts. Some people live here at their own expense, but this is permitted only to the sons of earls and barons or the eldest sons of the nobility. The colleges have stewards called Seneschals who are responsible for the catering.

The Masters of these colleges get the most magnificent treatment: they live in tremendous state and when they entertain it is with a whole troop of servants. Senior members of the colleges are called Fellows: if they should leave they get a farewell gift from the college of one hundred English pounds, i.e. 333 crowns. The Professors give barely thirty lectures a year, but these

*f.152*

8. Queens'
9. Jesus
10. Catharine's
11. Christ's
12. John's
13. Magdalene

14. Trinity
15. Emmanuel

16. Sidney

College revenues

College Masters

Senior members of the colleges

University Professors

*Cambridge, from John Caius' 'De antiquitate Cantabrigiensis Academiae', 1574. This map by Richard Lyne is schematic rather than accurate, with the colleges drawn too large, but it clearly shows the town's layout: at the northern end is the Castle, at the southern end Peterhouse, where Waldstein was entertained by Dr Soame. King's College Chapel is prominent in the centre. Garrett Hostel Green, over which Trinity and St John's were feuding (p. 103), was an island, centre left. (By permission of the Syndics of Cambridge University Library)*

lectures are very learned and are most meticulously prepared. Junior members, until they have taken a degree, must walk, when in the college grounds, with their hats off if they are in the presence of anyone who has graduated as a Master.

The highest position of all in the University is held by the Earl of Essex, and he has his Vice-Chancellor who is elected annually. Wherever the Vice-Chancellor goes he has the distinction of being preceded by 5 Bedels (they have 6 at Oxford) with silver-gilt maces. These Bedels are taken from the ranks of the gentry, and they get an annual salary of 200 English pounds. They wear silk gowns, and some (as at Oxford) even wear chains of office.   *Vice-Chancellor*   *Bedels*

By great good luck we happened to arrive at the very time when they celebrate the annual Promotions (they themselves call it Commencement). They have a number of different degrees: first they are made Sophist minors, and then Sophist majors; then come the Bachelors, who after their seventh year are considered fit to proceed to the degree of Master. (They make so much of this degree that they consider it an honour even for the noblest persons: they even have Masters in the place of noblemen, nor will they admit anyone who does not hold this degree to take part in their Congregations.)   *Grades of degree*   *Masters*

*f.153* After the Theological Candidates have completed 12 years from the taking of their Master's degree, they are awarded their Doctorates. The Promotor is called the 'father', the candidate is his 'son'. Two days are allotted to the Promotions: during the morning of the first day each Professor gives a special lecture to a selected audience on some brilliant and carefully worked out   *Method of conferring the degrees*

147 The practice of defending a thesis by disputation still continues in many Continental universities; it began to be abandoned in Cambridge during the early years of the nineteenth century as it was being completely superseded by the Senate House Examinations (i.e. the Tripos), and eventually became something of a farce. The last disputation for the B.A. degree at Cambridge took place in 1838.

For the heated discussion between Dr Overall (who maintained that until Christ's Ascension the Patriarchs were 'in Abraham's bosom' rather than in Heaven proper) and the orthodox, and his discomfiture witnessed by Waldstein, see the next day's Diary entry and note 152.

148 Robert Soame (frequently spelt 'Some') was Master of Peterhouse, and this was his third Vice-Chancellorship. He was a great controversialist and must have had a bold sense of humour, for on one occasion when he had been reproved by John Whitgift, Archbishop of Canterbury, for having preached too violently partisan a sermon, he next preached at Great St Mary's on Acts 4: 6, 7: 'Annas the High Priest, and Caiaphas, and *John* ... set them in the midst and asked "By what power or by what means have ye done this?"'

149 Probably in what is now the Old Schools, as at the time Great St Mary's was already occupied with the Masters of Arts' and the Bachelors' Commencements. (See *Churchwardens' Accounts of St Mary the Great*, ed. J. E. Foster, p. 264)

150 Waldstein had been entertained in the Master's rooms just above. The 'downstairs room' was known as the Stone Parlour; in 1870 it was united with some adjacent rooms to make the present Combination Room. The old portaits are now in the hall, Combination Room, and Parlour, but the Latin couplets, painted on separate panels beneath them, disappeared in the eighteenth century (my thanks to Dr David Watkin of Peterhouse for this information). They are recorded in the manuscript of the Rev. William Cole, reprinted in R. Willis and J. W. Clark's *Architectural History of the University of Cambridge*, Cambridge, 1886, I, pp. 63–68. The couplet beginning 'Prosunt' is not listed there; the others refer to John Holbroke, Master of Peterhouse (1430), Simon Langham, Bishop of Ely (1395), Sir Edward North (1564), and Dr Shirton, Master of Pembroke (1530).

Waldstein quotes only one line of the first couplet: 'Usury and the foul viper give birth in the same fashion.' (Contemporary belief, referred to in Sir Philip Sidney's *Apology for Poetry*, held that vipers 'with their birth kill their parents'.) The second line read: 'Qui juvat afflictos, foenerat ille Deo' – 'He who succours the afflicted, lends at interest to God'.

Waldstein copied out four other distichs as if they were one single poem, and admittedly they do appear to make a coherent sense. Each couplet is here translated in four lines.

> What decorates the budding years
>   As learning, which we now acclaim?
> What so consoles the old, and gives
>   A shelter from an evil name?

> If what is noble merits praise
>   The noblest thing deserves it most;
> And learning, nobler than all else
>   Should first deserve our happy boast.

theme. The afternoon is allotted to the disputations and declamations of the candidates.

At these disputations the presiding official is called the 'Moderator'. He begins by announcing the theme of the disputation and explaining what points are at issue: then, after the disputation is over it is he who gives the final judgment; produces reasons in support of his decision; and refutes and demolishes any outstanding arguments of the opposing candidates.

We did not see what happened on the first day of this annual ceremony, however, as it was already after sunset when we arrived, but nonetheless we did discover that there had been a tremendous dispute among the Professors, one of whom had hotly maintained that until Christ's Ascension the Patriarchs were not in Heaven but in some other place; on the following day another Moderator made a long speech and publicly refuted him.

TUESDAY, 11 JULY
In the morning we went to Peterhouse and presented ourselves before the Vice-Chancellor Robert Soame who welcomed us very graciously; afterwards we were taken to the place where Doctors' degrees are conferred.

Peterhouse is the oldest of the colleges. We saw, written on the wall in a downstairs room, the following well-turned verses:

>    *Partus dant similes usura et vipera foeda*

also:

>    *Laus pueris doctrina, decus florentibus annis*
>       *Solamen senio, perfugiumque malis.*
>    *Nobilis hic vere, vere si nobilis ullus*
>       *Qui sibi principium nobilitatis erat.*

> To over-eat and over-sleep
>    Will mark us with their weakening taint,
> So let us use them for the cause
>    With wholly admirable restraint.
>
> Who rightly fears the law of God
>    Lives ever near Him, in His sight;
> But he before Him worthy stands
>    Who learns the things he knows are right.

I have to thank Professor Dominique de Turville, himself a Peterhouse man, for this wholly admirable translation.

151  At the time Peterhouse had one of the best libraries of printed books in the whole of England. It had been bequeathed by Andrew Perne, Dean of Ely and Master of the College before Soame.

*Prosunt, si moderare, duo: lectusque cibusque,*
*Haec te debilitant, ni moderare, duo.*
*Proximus ille Deo qui paret recta monenti,*
*Dignus at ille Deo qui sibi recta sapit.*

The library here is the most famous of all the college libraries.

During the morning we saw 4 Doctors of Theology obtaining their degrees. They came forward into the middle of the assembly wearing scarlet gowns trimmed with white fur, and the Promotor – or 'father' – first of all told them to advance to the chair, which represents Licence to Teach. Then he placed upon each of their heads a flat cap, black and with four corners, symbolizing Theological Truth. Finally he embraced them with a kiss, which signifies Peace, Mutual Love, and Unity of Mind, and gave them the third gift: rings, which indicate the dignity of their appointment.

*The ceremony of creating Doctors of Theology*

(The following passage should have been placed earlier.)

When this had ended the disputations began. A very clever young man – one of those who were taking their Master's degrees that day – had undertaken to give replies to the propositions. He began with a brilliant little speech, first of all explaining the theological points at issue (there were two of these: the Presence of Christ in the Sacrament, and Justification by Faith) and then proving the chief objections of the adversaries to be unsound. His own opinions he gave to his audience in verse. After he had finished, first the Promotor or 'father', and then the newly-created Doctors his 'sons', produced arguments on the other side, and if they were found to be

*The method of holding disputations*

152 This colleague was Dr Overall, Regius Professor of Divinity and Master of my own College of St Catharine, then known as Catharine Hall. Waldstein heard only the final passage of a dispute which had lasted for some time; the rest of the story is revealed in letters and papers sent to Cecil by Vice-Chancellor Soame (Hatfield House Papers, x, pp. 208–12).

Cambridge was staunchly (even aggressively) Protestant in opinion, and during the past year Dr Overall's Professorial lectures had been criticized for their tendency towards what was considered to be Papist rather than orthodox Anglican doctrine. The Vice-Chancellor wanted to clear the matter up, and arranged for a discussion between Dr Overall and two other theologians, who were to represent the orthodox viewpoint. Sixteen questions of doctrine were discussed, and in eight of these cases Dr Overall found himself unable to agree with the appointees. Among the disputed doctrines which he upheld was that before the Ascension of Christ the souls of the Patriarchs were in Abraham's bosom, but not in Heaven proper. (I have it on the highest authority, Anglican *and* Episcopal, that Dr Overall's opinion, based on the teaching of the Early Church, was theologically valid.)

At a meeting on 4 June the Vice-Chancellor read out the orthodox doctrine on the eight disputed questions and invited Dr Overall to join in the acknowledgment of those doctrines. He refused, and was forbidden to pronounce publicly on any of the points.

Here the affair ought to have ended, but on the day of Waldstein's arrival in Cambridge Dr Soame had himself been Moderator at the Divinity disputations. At the end of the proceedings he had 'determined of the last question against the Popish sort, soundly and conspicuously' and had then, unwisely, allowed the Bedel to call upon Dr Overall 'ad commendationem'. Dr Overall clearly felt that it was one thing to be silent about his opinions but quite another to stand up and endorse arguments and beliefs which he considered to be fallacious, and so far from commending the Moderator's reasoning he entered a vigorous refutation of it. 'The like was never done before and is flat against all order of disputation', wrote the exasperated Vice-Chancellor, who had to order Dr Overall to be silent, finishing the meeting by expressing the wish 'that Dr Overall had not nourished these errors and had forborne to publish them in that excellent assembly'.

Soame was not prepared to leave it at that: on the following day (the occasion which Waldstein describes) the Moderator was Dr Playfair, and when the ceremonies were almost over he brought up (doubtless on Soame's instructions) the subject of the previous day's disputation, and 'refuted Dr Overall's dealing the day before with such soundness, learning, and perspicuity as did greatly content and satisfy the assembly. If some of his speeches were somewhat sharp in regard of the matter, they which love the truth will bear a little with him because he dealt against him which had faulted both in matter and manner . . .'

Dr Overall's unorthodoxy does not seem to have affected his career, for he was subsequently made Bishop of Norwich. He was partly responsible for the translation of the Genesis-Kings portion of the Authorized Version of the Bible.

Soame's speech as Moderator of the Divinity disputations survives among the Hatfield House Papers, as does a letter from him to Cecil dated 22 July (x, p. 241), in which he refers once more to Overall, and then mentions Waldstein and his friends: 'The nobleman of Bohemia and his company were respected of me at our Commencement, according to your letter.'

153 A partial eclipse of the sun had taken place at about noon on the previous day. (I have to thank the omniscience of H.M. Nautical Almanac Office at the Royal Observatory for this information.)

overstepping the limits of the debate or were being in any way irrelevant, then the Moderator interposed his authority and brought them back to the matter in hand with a warning not to use the weapons of Rhetoric and not to beat the air.

This lasted from 10 until one o'clock, when the Moderator began to sum up the main arguments and to wind up the debate by supporting the correct opinion with a number of apt quotations. Then, just as he seemed about to bring the whole thing to a conclusion, he reintroduced the main points of yesterday's disputation and made a most violent attack upon his colleague (the one who had conferred degrees upon the new Doctors). He belittled his theory concerning the Patriarchs, he undermined his arguments, and then he pressed home his own point with so much animus that the other man went quite red with mortification and might perhaps have spoken to defend himself if time had allowed.

As we had remained there until three o'clock without having had anything to eat, the Vice-Chancellor took us back home with him and ordered us an excellent lunch; and while we fortified our bodies, those who were just about to get their Master's degrees enjoyed an excellent meal for the mind, for during this time they heard a number of really worthwhile and enjoyable speeches and arguments, most particularly from one of the opponents called the Prevaricator, who wittily and with quite amusing jokes made fun of, and at the same time gave instruction to, the man who was replying to the argument.

These things went on for some time, and then at last the Masters (who were wearing liripipes) had their

> This Moderator, when one person was attacking, another, 'Don't' (he said) 'fight him with the spears of Rhetoric, but stab him with the dagger of argument.'

> Make a note of the eclipse.

154   'Master, come forward to be sworn.

Put your hand into the hand of the Master, and give your solemn undertaking that you will observe the established statutes, privileges, and customs of this University.

Lay your hand upon the Book. You shall swear, in your own person, that as God may help you in Jesus Christ you will take upon yourself the oath which, in his own person, the Master who swore earlier promised to maintain.

You will determine in private with a Master presiding.

Go forth.'

This was the shortened form of the oath, used when there was a large number of candidates. The first candidate ('the Master who swore earlier') had been sworn in full: his oath was to serve the five-year regency (period of compulsory residence for those who had proceeded to the M.A. degree), not to incept or lecture at any other university (except at Oxford), nor to allow persons who had incepted elsewhere to be admitted to any University faculty.

The order to 'determine' (i.e. perform a final disputation or exercise) was a survival from the time when further disputations followed the granting of degrees.

Miss E. S. Leedham-Green, of Cambridge University Archives, very kindly helped me with her knowledge of the subject and took both time and trouble in unearthing details of the degree oaths of the period.

155   This was permissible on such occasions, by University Ordnance 28 of Queen Mary's reign: 'it shall . . . be allowed at the time of taking degrees and of the fair at Stourbridge, for respectable women to dine or sup in the colleges, but not at the expense of the college and by no means to spend the night there.'

156   I have not been able to find any confirmation of this story; if Edward III did ever winter at Cambridge it might well have been at the King's Hall (subsequently part of Trinity), which he had founded and of which he himself was sole Visitor.

157           To Christopher Morley, formerly a Fellow of this College
                  This inscription was placed by John Sledd,
                    Former Fellow of the same College.

degrees conferred. Their number on this occasion exceeded one hundred and fifty. We made a special point of asking for the form of words used in creating each Master to be written down for us. It runs as follows, word for word:

*Magister incipe ad oppositum: pone manum in manum Magistri, et fac fidem de servando statuta, privilegia, consuetudines huius Universitatis approbatas: pone manum super Leibrum: item proesta iuramentum quod praestitit olim Magister, in sua persona, praestabis tu in tua sic te DEUS adiuvet in Jesu Christo. Quaestionem determinabis in aurem magistro sedendo. EXEITO.*

<small>Formula for creating Masters</small>

When the whole ceremony was over we followed the Vice-Chancellor back to Peterhouse where a banquet had been prepared: they even had ladies present among the guests. (Members of the colleges usually celebrate by feasting together when one of their number has a degree conferred, and since there was such a crowd of candidates nearly every college was having a banquet.) We were given a splendid welcome (this is usual with the English where foreigners are concerned) and were most courteously entertained; we then went back to our lodging.

WEDNESDAY, 12 JULY
Spent the day in seeing the colleges. First we went to Trinity which is the largest of them all: in it one can still see the house where Edward the Third and his Queen spent a whole winter. In the chapel where the prayers and services are held is this epitaph:

<small>Trinity College</small>

*Christophoro Morle huius collegii quondam socio posuit Joannes Slede, ibidem quondam socius.*

> With solemn black the stage is hung,
> Music is silent, hushed each tongue,
> For dead lies Morley, our delight.
>
> But yet, you have not perished. We,
> Heirs to your language, hearing, sight,
> Shall we ourselves not be
> Your music, speech, and scenery?
>
> To such a life, give the applause that's due!
> And be his works by every age kept new.
>
> William Alabaster mourned him.
> Died AD 1596, 18 April.

William Alabaster, Fellow of Trinity (1589) and author of the successful tragedy *Roxana*, had been chaplain to Essex on the Cadiz expedition.

Christopher Morley's epitaph – along with many others – probably disappeared, so the College Librarian informed me, when the chapel was reconstructed early in the eighteenth century. No dramatic works by Morley are known to exist: they were probably Latin plays which were performed by members of the College.

158 'Beaumont, Master of the College, gave this and some books on Divinity; he steadfastly forbade the toleration of Papist practices.'

Robert Beaumont, Master of Trinity 1561–67, was a prominent and inflexible Puritan. In addition to the books referred to he also left to the College the fine picture of Henry VIII which now hangs in the hall.

159 The dispute had broken out in the previous year, 1599. The controversial piece of land (now part of Trinity Backs) was a portion of waste ground known as Garret Hostel Green, just to the north of where Garret Hostel Lane now runs. Trinity's plan to enclose this ground for their own use was hotly contested by St John's College. The Queen's decision in favour of Trinity was not quite the end of the affair, and Trinity did not gain full possession of Garret Hostel Green until 1612.

(Detailed accounts of this dispute, derived from documents in the Public Record Office and from the Harleian Papers, are given in the Trinity College entry of Willis and Clark's *Architectural History of the University of Cambridge* (see note 150) and in *The Eagle* (St John's College, Cambridge), XXXI. I have to thank Mr N. C. Buck of St John's College Library for drawing my attention to these sources.)

160 Whitaker had died five years previously; he had been appointed to the Mastership of St John's College by the Crown against the wishes of a number of Fellows who suspected him of overmuch puritanism, but he fully justified his appointment and the College prospered under his wise and equable rule.

Waldstein's description of him as 'exceedingly learned' was no exaggeration: Whitaker was regarded as the intellectual champion of the Church of England just as Cardinal Bellarmine was regarded as the champion of the Church of Rome. Cooper's *Athenae Cantabrigienses* records that Bellarmine privately much admired Whitaker and kept his picture in his study: when his Jesuit friends enquired why, he would answer 'that although he was an heretic, and his adversary, yet he was a learned adversary'.

The epitaph which Waldstein records is incised on a black marble tablet which is now in the College ante-chapel. The lettering, once gilded, has now become most inconspicuous and needs to be restored. It reads, translated:

'Here lies Doctor Whitaker, late Regius Professor of Divinity, skilled as a linguist, acute as a critic, a man of acknowledged dignity and prudence, untiring in toil and of unblemished life. United to these gifts he possessed that rarest of virtues among such talents, a marked humility of mind. He was for the space of eight years a wise Master of this College, an upholder of goodness, a foe to all evil.'

*f.156*
> Squallet scena, silent linguae, nec Musica garrit
>     Delicium ut nostrum Morlius interiit:
> Sed non interiisti, oculis, ore, auribus haeres
>     Nosque erimus linguae, musica, scena tibi.
> Plaudite cui talis transacta est fabula vitae
>     Posteritas semper quam facit esse novam.
>
>     Wilhelmus Alabaster deflevit
>     Obiit anno Domini 1596. 18 April:

Above the pulpit and lectern one can see the inscription:

> Beaumontus praeses dedit, atque volumina sacra
> Duntaxat voluit vetuitque papistica ferre.

158

There is a good deal of ill-feeling between this college and St John's: it is all about some piece of meadow land, but the Queen has given her decision in favour of Trinity.

159

Later we went to St John's College. At one time it had the very famous and exceedingly learned theologian Whitaker as Master. His memorial is in the chapel with this inscription:      John's College

> Hic situs est Doctor WITAKERUS regius olim
> Scripturae interpres, quem ornabat gratia linguae,
> Judiciique acies, et lucidus ordo memorque
> Pectus, et invictus labor et sanctissima vita
> Una sed enituit virtus rarissima, tantas
> Ingenii inter opes, submissio candida mentis
> Huius Gymnasii super annos octo Magister
> Providus, et recti defensor, et ultor iniqui.

160

This college has the most delightful and beautifully laid out grounds and open spaces adjoining.

Next we went to Magdalene College; 'GARDE TA      Magdalene College

161 The motto (together with the arms of the College) is not over the main entrance gate but above the gateway which now leads from the main court to the Pepys Library. Both motto and arms are taken from the family of Sir Thomas Audley, the founder.

162 A survey of Cambridge Castle dated six years later (8 July 1606) which has, writes W. M. Palmer, 'the appearance of having at some time been crumpled up and stuffed into a hole in the wall to keep out the wind and rain', states: 'There remaineth the Gatehouse used as a common Gaol and dwelling of the Gaoler. All the rest of the walls of the Castle and their foundations are razed and utterly ruinated saving a parcel of wall on the N.W. side...' (from *Cambridge Castle*, in Cambridge University Library)

163 This tower was the original Castle gatehouse. There were twenty prisoners in custody when Hentzner visited Cambridge two years previously.

164 Building had begun in 1595 and the College had opened for its first students in 1598.

165 The 'dissertation by Wolfius' could not, in spite of an intensive search by the Librarian of Emmanuel College, be traced either in the Library or in any of the early catalogues.
  The copy of Cicero's *De Officiis*, on the other hand, is still in the Library. It is a magnificent example of very early printing on vellum, printed in Mainz in 1465. It originally belonged to Prince Arthur, elder brother of Henry VIII, and the first page of each of its four books was decorated *c.* 1500 with the Prince's coat-of-arms and with flowers. No one knows how it came into the possession of the College. (See colour plate IV.)

166 Eagle lecterns were at that time almost unknown on the Continent; the splendid example in St Mark's, Venice, and the one in the Cathedral at Urbino are both of English workmanship.
  The fifteenth-century lectern in Christ's chapel is believed to have belonged to God's House, the original hall which Lady Margaret Tudor refounded as Christ's College.

167 The coats-of-arms are unlikely to have been those of other colleges. They were probably the arms of the founder and of benefactors.

168 Huge as King's Chapel is, it is not this long: the internal length of the vault is 296 feet (90.2 m).

169 This Psalter had originally belonged to the great scholar Jerónimo Osorio, Bishop of Sylves. The Bishop's library was plundered by Essex during the raid of 1596. Sir William Monson, who commanded the *Repulse* on the expedition, wrote in his memoirs (pub. Navy Records Society, London, 1902): 'The only thing that was afterwards attempted was Faro, a town of Algarve in Portugal, a place of no resistance or wealth, only famous for the library of Osorius who was Bishop of that see; which library was brought into England by us, and many of the books bestowed upon the new-erected library of Oxford' (see below, note 211). The success of the Cadiz expedition brought Essex to the utmost height of popular acclaim: the eulogy inscribed in the Psalter does not in the least exaggerate the hero-worship felt for him by the nation as a whole.
  The late A. N. L. Munby, Librarian of King's, replied to my enquiry about 'a large Psalter from Cadiz with an introductory poem' telling me that the book was still in the possession of the College. He added: 'I suppose it is too much to hope that your diarist made a copy of the verses, as the first two pages of the book have long been missing.'

161 FOY' is written up on the wall over the entrance gate. Close by is the castle; it was built by Canute, King of
162 the Danes, but is now demolished. From it, 10 miles off, one can see the cathedral of Ely. The Court of Law which serves all the county is beside this castle, and not far off there is a tower where prisoners are kept in chains
163 until they are tried.

164 We then visited the new college called 'Sidney', which is very fine with a particularly splendid hall. After seeing all this we went back to our inn where we had been invited for lunch with the Vice-Chancellor by one of the new Doctors. *Sidney College*

In the afternoon we saw Emmanuel College which is also a very attractive place: in its library they have a dissertation by Wolfius with Greek lettering and numerals, and also a copy of Cicero's *De Officiis* printed
f.157 almost as soon as the printing press was invented. Then
165 to Christ's College which has a most delightful orchard;
166 in their college chapel the lectern is a brass eagle. *Emmanuel College*

*Christ's College*

Last of all (leaving out the other more ordinary colleges) we went to King's, which is more splendid than any of the others; it has the painted coats-of-arms of
167 the other colleges displayed along its outside walls. But above all is its chapel, which is lovely and is kingly indeed. It is built like a palace, it has the imposing length of 150 yards, being filled with light from stained
168 glass windows. Close to the chapel is the library: this contains a notable Book of the Psalms five spans in height, which the Earl of Essex brought back from Cadiz near the Straits of Gibraltar where the crossing
169 from Spain to Africa is shortest. On the first page the following verses are written: *King's College*

*What volume are you, and whose? Whence come you?* I am a Spaniard.
*From the wreck of Cadiz? and an enemy?* Rather, call me a stranger.
*Tell me, then, stranger: what fortune has carried you here to our shores?*
It was the fortune of war. *Who waged it?* A force out of England.
*Do then your pages proclaim the way that war was conducted?*
That is a task more fit for the English: no such duty is mine:
Never let book like mine tell the English (my witness is truthful)
Those many war-exploits of which I could give an account.
*Tell me at least: who led the assault? – no Spaniard can hear you.*
That indeed I can say, even though men count it as treason:
   The whole wide world is aware how they ravaged the town of Cadiz,
For what man never heard tell of that fearful grappling with Spain
That famed Peninsular raid, which, under command of a hero
– Greater than Hercules he – came right to Hercules' Pillars!
He (and in proverbs now, his name personifies valour)
Who is the friend and beloved of the common people of England,
Head and shoulders above the rest in height and in honours,
Who held all menacing Spain in check, at the sack of Cadiz.
   Then, when the Englishmen carried away the best of the treasures,
Myself formed one little part of the plunder obtained from the Church.
And therefore I curse the Briton, who carries away to his homeland
The wealth of the Indies: the boast of ever-unsatisfied Ebro.
*Tell me, who placed you here? and why? and when did he bring you?*
My comrades and I were brought by one of Faldon's companions
To be a glorious token, recording a glorious triumph,
In the November that followed after Cadiz was destroyed.
Phoebus already had followed his course some thirty and nine times
On that sceptre of might, which long may Elizabeth wield.
*But what do your fetters imply?* They prevent me from ever escaping;
See! the unyielding chain is riveted into my side.
This is my homeland to me: I once 'Cantaber' was called,
But by a change of name am I 'Cantabricus' now;
And what the whole Spanish world was once unable to hold
Now King's College contains in its humble library walls.
   And now, this only I fear, that some Englishman cut me in pieces,
And that, to the English I trust, will reverence and kindness forbid.
Spare me therefore I pray (I have felt enough wounds in the past),
Do not harm yet more the defenceless skin of a captive.

The identity of 'Faldon' is a mystery to me; the Latin word is 'Faldonis', so the name could perhaps be Fald or Faldow. None of the commanders on the Cadiz expedition had a name resembling this.

   The volume was rebound in oak boards during the nineteenth century and is no longer chained.

*Quid tu quaeso liber? cuius? Hispanus, at unde?*
    *Gadibus a laceris, hostis? at hospes ego*
*Tunc hospes quae te sors nostris appulit oris?*
    *Bellica: quis bellum hoc gesserat? Angla cohors.*
*An scripto narras gesti praeconia belli?*
    *Anglorum potius non meus iste labor.*
*Ingleis quale meum (fateor nam vera) volumen*
    *Non ferat ut pangat tot bene gesta capax.*
*Quo duce dic saltem, nullus te Cantaber audit*
    *Hoc etiam patria vel renuente loquar.*
*Cui non audita est Gandensis fama ruinae?*
    *Cui non Hispanis illa tremenda manus?*
*Hispanis laudanda manus, quam duxerat heros*
    *Usque Herculeas Hercule maior aquas.*
*Ille (sed in dicto designat nomine virtus)*
    *Angliacae magnus plebis amorque comas.*
*Qui vertice omnes et celso vertice supra est*
    *Continet Hispanas Gade ruente minas.*
*Atque hinc exuvias Anglo asportante superbas*
    *De templi spoliis pars ego parva fui.*
*Sic precor et patriam quamvis male transferat Anglus*
    *Indas quas avidus iactat Iberus opes.*
*Verum hic te posuit quis? cur et quando locavit?*
    *Mecum Faldonis cum sociis socius.*
*Ut fierem insignis monumentum insigne triumphi*
    *Alter ab eversa Gade November erat.*
*Iamque potens Phoebo terter triciesque redacto*
    *Sceptrum quod longum gestat et ELISABETH.*
*At quid vincla volunt? ne ut quo discedere possit*
    *En fixa est lateri dura catena meo.*
*Ast haec mi patria est, fueram quod Cantaber ante*
    *Nunc quoque sum verso nomine Cantabricus.*
*Quam prius haud potuit retinere Hispanicus orbis*
    *Parvula regalis Bibliotheca tenet.*
*Tantum nunc metuo, ne quis me evisceret Anglus*
    *Quod pietas Anglis fausta qui opto vetet.*
*Parcite vos igitur (satis olim vulnera sensi)*
    *Nudam captivi dilacerate cutem.*

There are four separate rooms to this library. The College buildings are roofed with lead, and are decorated all round with very handsome columns.

*The brass eagle lectern, of late fifteenth-century date, in the chapel of Christ's College, Cambridge (see p. 105). (By kind permission of the Master and Fellows of Christ's College, Cambridge  Photo Emily Lane)*

170 It is actually nearly twice as far. Waldstein's descriptions of Godmanchester and Huntingdon are taken from Camden's *Britannia*.

171 This was no obsolete custom at the time of Waldstein's visit. When James I passed through Godmanchester, Stow's *Annals* records: 'the Bayliffes of the towne with their brethren met him, acknowledging their aleagiance, there conveying him through the towne, they presented him with three-score and ten teeme of horse, al traced to faire new Ploughes, in shew of their husbandry: which, while his Maiestie being very well delighted with the sight demaunded why they offered him so many Horses and Ploughes: he was answered, that it was their auncient custome, whensoever any King of England passed through their towne, so to present him.'

172 Nothing remains of this castle – formerly an important stronghold and the birthplace of Richard III – except for a large mound; it was destroyed by order of James I because it had been the place of his mother's execution in 1587.

173 The river is not the Avon but the Nene.

In the evening we dined in private with the Vice-Chancellor.

THURSDAY, 13 JULY
We left Cambridge in the morning at about nine o'clock, taking the road through the village of Godmanchester which lies 8 miles from Cambridge, near to — and in the county of — Huntingdon. It is a good large village, famous as an agricultural centre, situated upon light soil in an open plain with a southward facing slope.

There is nowhere in England, so they say, with so many hard-working farmers and so much land under the plough, and they pride themselves on the fact that Kings of England, when travelling this way, have been greeted with a procession of one hundred and eighty ploughs by way of a rural celebration.

We pushed on from here to Huntingdon, the county town, which is 12 miles from Cambridge. It is nobly — and at the same time attractively — situated; it lies in a piece of country which is surrounded by the Fens, it is alive with game and fish, and is far superior to any of the other towns in the neighbourhood. We stopped here for something to eat; then, making our way up north from here we did another 16 miles and came to the castle of Fotheringhay.

This castle is an extremely old one: it is built on a wide stretch of open ground among beautiful meadows and it is exceedingly picturesque with a most lovely river, the Avon, flowing by the castle and the fields around it. It was in this castle that Mary Stuart, Queen of Scotland, was kept prisoner, and here, after she had been

Fotheringhay Castle in which the Queen of Scotland was beheaded

174 This phrase presumably means that the verdict was a very popular one, as indeed it was. At the news of Mary's execution the bells were rung in London, fires were lighted in the streets, and there was much merry-making and banqueting.

175 There is no proof that Norfolk ever actually met the Queen of Scots, and so far from being accustomed 'to visit her every evening' he had been dead for fifteen years by the time of Mary's execution. He was beheaded in 1572 for supporting the Ridolfi Plot, which was to arrange an invasion of England by Spanish troops from the Netherlands simultaneously with an uprising of the English Catholics with a view to putting Mary on the English throne with himself as her consort.

176 This derivation of the town's name is taken from Camden.

177 The house had been completed only eleven years previously; it still presents very much the same splendid appearance that it did at the time of Waldstein's visit. (See Christopher Hussey's articles in *Country Life*, 3 and 10 December 1953.)

Burghley House. The entrance front is on the left. (Photo A. F. Kersting)

arraigned for high treason she was – by the verdict of the whole of England – condemned to death and beheaded with an axe. We saw the lower hall in which the execution took place and the upper hall where the sentence was pronounced, as well as the room where she was imprisoned. The Duke of Norfolk, who used to visit her every evening, by doing this had drawn suspicion upon himself and was executed beforehand.

After 6 more miles we came to Stamford, a well populated town in Lincolnshire which is built of stone (hence the name); it has been granted a number of privileges and is fortified with a wall. Here we slept the night.

FRIDAY, 14 JULY

From Stamford we went the 1 mile to see Burghley House, the seat of William Cecil the Lord Treasurer. People say of him that 'after climbing the ladder of success he pulled it well out of everyone else's reach': this is because he was raised to his own high rank after completing his studies, and ever afterwards he refused to allow any well-educated person to enter his department. Anyhow, the mansion which is built of square-cut stone is very splendid; the drive which leads up to the main entrance is an unusually long one and great care has been taken to choose the best sites for planting the trees on either side of it. There is an extremely rich garden, completely surrounded by a wall; beyond it, at the entrance to the mansion, there is a really fine fish-pond, and the great kitchen is a place fit to cook a banquet for a king. The hall is extremely large, its roof vaulted and most beautifully made: it contains pictures of Medea and

*Burghley the mansion of the Secretary*

178 Hatton had built himself a very splendid mansion indeed, which nearly bankrupted him. It was purchased in 1605 by James I; Charles I visited it several times and was kept prisoner there in 1647. Most of it was demolished in Parliamentary times. The original plans are now in Sir John Soane's Museum, London.

For an interesting description of this most palatial country seat, in the building of which Hatton deliberately set out to surpass the grandeur of Burghley's gorgeous Theobalds, see Mark Girouard's articles, 'Elizabethan Holdenby', *Country Life*, 18 and 25 October 1979.

Waldstein is wrong in saying that Holdenby was 'sometimes called Holborn'. It was alternatively known as 'Holmeby'. Waldstein, hearing that Hatton had owned a house in 'Holbrunna', assumed that this meant Holmeby; in fact *Holbrunna* (or *Holburna*) is Latin for Holborn, where Sir Christopher had his London residence (part of the area is still known as Hatton Garden). Hatton had died in his London house, and Waldstein repeats his mistake a few lines later when he writes 'it was here' (meaning Holdenby) 'that he died'.

179 One of these obelisks survived long enough to be reproduced in Buck's eighteenth-century engraving of the ruins of Holdenby.

Jason, and of Hector and Cassandra. Going up the stairs you see the names and coats-of-arms of some of the Garter Knights. In one of the rooms there is a chimney-piece made of the purest white marble: it is not unlike a looking-glass, and by natural reflection you can see the neighbouring countryside in it quite clearly when the windows are open – fields, trees, and towers as well. One of the bedrooms contains a bed of Indian workmanship with its coverlet embroidered in gold thread. All the chimneys are of quarried stone shaped like columns, and in one place 6 are joined together, making a buttress for the house.

*Note that small things in the great English houses are built to represent columns.*

There is an interesting water supply system near the kitchen: the water comes from quite a long way off and is brought through pipes to a considerable height. There is a promenade or gallery, with a leaden floor, from which you get a most beautiful view.

After leaving the mansion we made for the south and west of England. Passed the fort of Collyweston 2 miles out of Stamford, and at the village of Kettering, with Stamford 16 miles behind us, we stopped for lunch.

In 10 more miles we reached Holdenby (sometimes called Holborn) House, in Northamptonshire, a stately and most magnificent place built by a very illustrious knight, Sir Christopher Hatton, Privy Councillor and Lord Chancellor of England; he came of an old Holdenby family and it was here that he died. The house contains a very large number of rooms and windows, but no one is living there. Two stone obelisks stand by the 4 steps which lead up to the porch, and the door itself is quite enormously massive. Coming through this porch you enter the hall; when you go through it the general interior plan of the house is revealed.

*Holborn, seat of one of the Queen's councillors*

180     Fate had deprived me of my old domain
        But from its broken ruins, built up new,
        Another Fate gave back again
        This mansion which you view.
        Live, great Elizabeth, eternally!
        Free giver of such welcome toil to me.

   The verse refers to legal transactions between Hatton and the Queen. In 1568 Hatton made over his hereditary estate of the manor of Holdenby to the Queen in exchange for the abbey and lands of Sulby, but received from her at the same time a lease for forty years on the Holdenby estate. In 1570 she gave him back the freehold, and by doing so gave him the 'welcome toil' of being able to build a magnificent home upon his own family property. (See E. Hartshorne, *Memorials of Holdenby*, London, 1868, and E. St J. Brooks, Sir *Christopher Hatton*, London, 1946.)

181 Queen Elizabeth's personal motto, meaning 'Ever the Same'; and Hatton's, 'If Ultimately'.

182 The house was Althorp. Sir John Spencer had in fact died earlier that year, and was succeeded by his son, Sir Robert, who was created Baron Spencer of Wormleighton three years later. The Spencers were famous for their sheep farms, and Waldstein's figure is probably an underestimate: Sir Robert had over 2,500 sheep on his Northamptonshire property in April that year and 7,448 on his Warwickshire estate.
   I have to thank Mr P. I. King of the Northamptonshire Record Office for this and other information about the district.

183 The town walls of Northampton were demolished in 1662.

184 The 'ancient camp' is Hunsbury Hill. The information about the battle, and the opinion, are Camden's.

Inside the hall these lines are written above the door:

> *Eripuit sors vera mihi, sors altera reddit*
> *Haec loca, quae veteri, rudere structa vides.*
> *Aeternos vivat magna Elisabetha per annos*
> *Quae metam grato laeta labore beat.*

In one of the rooms, displayed on three tall obelisks, are the names and coats-of-arms of the earls, barons, and other noblemen who have their estates in the county. Beneath the royal arms is the motto 'Semper Eadem', and Hatton's own coat-of-arms has 'Tandem Si'.

The house contains a number of beautifully made and extremely valuable chimney-pieces: one of these depicts Apollo, the Nine Muses, and Athena and Mercury, all carved out of stone, with four columns on either side; another has Jupiter seated on an eagle and the Seven Liberal Arts. In the same room are the arms of the Earl of Leicester, with 'Droict et Loyal'.

Not far from this mansion there is a famous house belonging to a man named Sir John Spencer who is said to own 2,000 sheep.

We left here at sunset and covered the 4 miles on to Northampton, a town ringed with fortifications and surrounded, for as far as the eye can see, by an extensive plain. Westwards from here there is an ancient camp: in 1460 when England was torn in two with civil war this was the site of the disastrous battle in which King Henry the Sixth was taken prisoner by Richard Neville, Earl of Warwick.

SATURDAY, 15 JULY
Leaving Northampton early in the morning, we travelled the 8 miles of road through woodland country to

185 Because of its three bridges Towcester, which does indeed lie on a great Roman road (Watling Street, which led from London to Wroxeter), was long believed to have been Tripontium. It has now been identified as Lactodorum; Tripontium was some distance to the north.

186 Local inhabitants gave me the same information that the streams continue to flow even in the severest drought, but I could find no record of any petrifying stream or well in the neighbourhood.

187 Woodstock Palace lay on rising ground near the north end of the present bridge over the lake at Blenheim. The description of Woodstock is from Camden's *Britannia*; Camden cites the historian John Rosse as his authority. Hentzner quotes the same description.

Queen Elizabeth, who had good reason to dislike this palace, only rarely visited Woodstock after her accession, and its interior was probably a good deal less stately than the interior of any of her other palaces. Three years after Waldstein's visit, when James I stayed there, Robert Cecil wrote, presumably with some personal feeling: 'The King, regardless of the comfort of his courtiers, had it roughly fitted up for himself, while the household were obliged to lodge even in tents.'

Vanbrugh, architect of the present Blenheim Palace, showed himself much in advance of his time as a conservationist by pleading that the remnants of the old palace might be preserved in view of their historical associations. The Marlboroughs however refused, and the last remains of the Palace of Woodstock were demolished in 1723. (See Ian Dunlop, *Palaces and Progresses of Elizabeth I*.)

188 This is quite inaccurate. Elizabeth was brought to Woodstock in May 1554 and remained there as a prisoner only until April in the following year.

*Woodstock Palace as it stood in 1714. (Aquatint in the Bodleian Library, Oxford, GA Oxon a 110)*

185 Towcester, known in ancient times as Tripontium. Near the town there is a most unusual game-park where the trees have been trained into arbours. The old Roman Praetorian Way is said to have run through Towcester. Three streams intersect the place, the largest of them running outside the town and the two smaller ones flowing through it. Although these are quite shallow streams, according to the local inhabitants they never run dry, and they say that if a piece of wood is thrown into 186 one of them, then after a time it will turn into stone. Carrying straight on through here, after 8 miles we came to Brackley where we lunched.

In such places the green boughs of the trees are woven into shelters where huntsmen hide to shoot the game which wanders about the place

In the afternoon we turned some 6 miles off our route to the Palace of Woodstock, which is a very extensive 187 royal residence built by Henry the First. He gave it a large park surrounded by a stone wall, the first of its kind in England according to historians. The royal domain lies in a valley where a brook wanders lazily through meadows, all very picturesquely; the palace itself is sited on a mound in order to give a better view of the surrounding hills and closely wooded country.

Woodstock Palace

The palace buildings are rectangular in plan with a huge open courtyard in the centre, and there is one spot in this courtyard where, if you stand and shout, the echo sends you back a reply four or five times over. The thing above all to see in this palace is the room in which the present Queen Elizabeth was kept prisoner for a whole 188 four years by order of her sister Mary. Even now one can read her verses in English, written on the wall in Elizabeth's own handwriting. They are as follows:

*Oh Fortune, thy wresting wavering state*
*Hath fraught with cares my troubled wit,*

189 The lines were first printed in Hentzner's Diary in 1612. They appear in a very mangled version indeed, as neither Hentzner nor (obviously) his Nuremberg printer knew any English. Bentley tried to make some sense out of Hentzner's transcription but is very far from Elizabeth's original poem. Leicester Bradner (*The Poems of Queen Elizabeth I*, Brown University, 1964) reconstructed the original lines with only one error: in line 4 he reads 'where once was love's loan quit'.

'Much suspected by me' i.e. concerning me.

190 Eisenberg noted in 1614: 'you see here the verses written with a diamond on a window by Queen Elizabeth'. He does not quote any of them, however, and perhaps recounts only what he was told had once been written there.

191 The story of Fair Rosamund was copied from Camden's *Britannia*. Her father was Sir Walter Clifford; his wife and their daughter Rosamund were both buried in the nunnery at Godstow which he endowed. Rosamund had become the mistress of Henry II at the time when his Queen, the famous Eleanor of Aquitaine, was in custody for her part in the revolt of some of the French dependencies against her husband.

Fair Rosamund clearly had the kind of personality to which myths adhere and accrue. Stories of the maze, later of the silken clue, later still of the cup of poison, and finally of the poison-or-dagger choice, are subsequent additions to her life-story without any discoverable basis in fact.

The historian Roger de Hoveden relates that Hugh, Bishop of Lincoln, strongly objected to her splendid tomb being venerated before the altar of Godstow nunnery church (it is easy to account for its presence there since Henry II had granted special privileges to the nunnery where her body lay), saying: ' "Take her away from here for she was a harlot: and bury her outside of the church with the rest, that the Christian religion may not grow into contempt, and that other women, warned by her example, may abstain from illicit and adulterous intercourse", which was accordingly done.' Rosamund was duly reburied, not exactly 'with the rest' but in the chapter house, where her tomb remained until it was destroyed at the Reformation. [continued on p. 120]

> *Whose witness this present prison late*
> *Could bear, where once was joy flown quite.*
> *Thou causedst the guilty to be loosed*
> *From lands where innocents were enclosed,*
> *And caused the guiltless to be reserved,*
> *And freed those that death had well deserved.*
> *But all herein can be naught wrought;*
> *So God grant to my foes as they have thought.*
>     *Finis. Elisabeth a prisoner.* 1555
> *Much suspected by me, but nothing proved can be.*

which is, in Latin:

> *O fortuna tuus nimium contortus status*
> *Adimplevit curis mentem turbulentem,*
> *Cuius in testimonium hic nuperus improvisus carcer*
> *Potuit ferre, tunc demum cum gaudium fuit omne ereptum.*
> *Tu nos vinculis exemisti tum cum innocentes erant*
> *Inclusi, soepe etiam innocentes servasti.*
> *At tamen ex hoc certi nihil potest concludi;*
> *Tandem sic Deus rependat inimicis meis*
> *Uti mihi facere cogitaverunt.*
>     *Elisabetha*
> *Multa suspicantur de me, sed nihil probatur.*

They say that she wrote other things too with a diamond on one of the windows, but these inscriptions no longer exist.

The ancient circular chapel here is also well worth seeing, and near the palace are the remains of the house where Rosamund Clifford, the mistress of Henry II, is said to have lived.

According to the historians Henry II fell madly in love with Rosamund Clifford who was so outstandingly beautiful and gracious that her loveliness wiped every other woman right out of the King's mind; she was already known everywhere as 'Rosa mundi', and to hide her from the malice of his Juno of a wife he had a

The rhyming and punning epitaph was probably added to the tomb at the time of its removal: its half-hostile tone reflects St Hugh's disapproval.

> The Rose of the World, though a rose not unsullied
> lies here in the tomb
> Foul-scented; who once was accustomed to render
> so sweet a perfume.

The epitaph was well known and is mentioned by Holinshed, who refers us to the translation in Richard Grafton's *Chronicles of England*, but Grafton is far too moralistic in his rendering:

> Though she were sweete, nowe fowly doth she stinke
> A myrrour good for all that on her thinke.

192 The account of Oxford is taken from Camden's *Britannia*, and the list of the colleges from the same unidentified source which was used by Hentzner. Waldstein has transcribed Camden's account almost verbatim, only omitting here and there a sentence which he considers unimportant.

193 'An abode of the Muses and a stronghold.'

An impression of Oxford from the south-east. The tall spire on the left is Christ Church, the tower in the centre left Merton, the next tall tower Magdalen, and the two spires to the right of it All Saints and St Mary the Virgin. (Detail of Joris Hoefnagel's view, from 'Civitates Orbis Terrarum' by Braun and Hogenberg)

labyrinth constructed within the building, full of
winding paths and confusing turnings running
backwards and forwards. No traces of it now remain.
This Rosamund is buried in the town of Godstow, three
miles away, with the following rhymed epitaph:

> *Hic iacet in tumba Rosa mundi, non Rosamunda;*
> *Non redolet sed olet, quae redolere solet.*

We left here for Oxford which is 6 miles from Woodstock and arrived in the evening.

Oxford has the most famous university in England, μουσεῖον and ἔρεισμα. It is a noble and distinguished city from every point of view, whether you have in mind the beauty of its private buildings, or the dignity of its public ones, or the healthiness and charm of its situation. Wooded hills make a rampart about its level plain, protecting it on the one side from the plague-bearing south wind, and on another from the stormy west, but leaving it open to the east wind which brings fine weather, and to the north which keeps away infectious diseases.

Richard the First, King of England, was born here. Robert d'Oilly, a Norman noble, received estates in this district as a reward for his military services, and built a massive lofty castle in the western part of the city; it is believed that he also built new fortifications round the city itself, but these are now being slowly destroyed in their battle with time. Even in those days there existed the very ancient Academy which the Popes of Rome had long before honoured with the title of 'University' at a time when they considered no others worthy of the name except for Paris and Padua.

194 Both University College and Balliol College, founded, according to the Oxford University Calendar, in 1249 and 1263 respectively, claim priority over Merton. Merton was in fact founded in 1264 and moved to Oxford in 1274.

195 Hart Hall was not founded by Walter Stapleton. It was a hostel of the late thirteenth century, the property of Elias de Hertford, and probably carried the sign of a hart's head as depicted upon Elias' private seal (a hart's head with a cross between the antlers).

Hart Hall was then sold to Stapleton for his foundation of Exeter College; it was also used by William of Wykeham for his scholars (already incorporated) while New College was being built. Although for a long time it was an adjunct of Exeter College, Hart Hall preserved its own identity and eventually became Hertford College.

196 A number of the colleges mentioned changed their name or merged with others: King's became known as Oriel, and St Mary's Hall was absorbed into it; Canterbury was on the site of the Canterbury Quadrangle of Christ Church; Durham became Trinity; Gloucester became Worcester; and St Bernard's became St John's.

There are 16 colleges and 8 halls.

The oldest college is Merton. Walter Merton, Bishop of Rochester, founded the College in Surrey in 1274 during the reign of Henry III. He moved it to Oxford, endowed it, and named it Merton College.

Next is University College, founded by Alfred, and immediately afterwards rebuilt by William, Archdeacon of Durham.

In the reign of Edward the First Balliol College was founded and named by John Balliol, King of Scotland. It is estimated that it had thirty Oxford students at the time.

Under Edward the Second, Exeter College and Hart Hall were founded by Walter Stapleton, Bishop of Exeter. The King himself followed his example, founding King's College and St Mary's Hall.

Next were Queen's College, founded by Philippa, wife of Edward III; Canterbury by Simon Islip, Archbishop of Canterbury; and soon afterwards William Wykeham, Bishop of Winchester, founded the splendid college known as New College. Then followed Durham College, founded by Thomas Hatfield, Bishop of Durham, and Lincoln College, intended for monks, by Richard Fleming, Bishop of Lincoln. During this same period the Benedictine monks contributed money for the foundation of Gloucester College.

In the following century under Henry V, Chichele, Archbishop of Canterbury, built two splendid colleges, one of which he dedicated to the memory of All Souls, and the other to the Blessed St Bernard. Immediately after this William Wayneflete, Bishop of Winchester, founded the College of Mary Magdalen, nobly built, on

There are 16 Oxford colleges

1. Merton

2. University

3. Balliol

4. Exeter

5. King's
6. Queen's College
7. Canterbury

8. New
9. Durham
10. Lincoln

11. Gloucester

12. All Souls'
13. St Bernard's

14. Mary Magdalen's

197 Zeuxis was a famous Greek painter of the fifth century B C, who is known to have been, apparently with good reason, very proud of his own paintings. The quotation, which means 'Easier to carp at than to copy', is a slight variant of what Zeuxis wrote beneath his painting, *The Athlete*. (See Pliny, *Natural History*, xxxv, 63.)

Duke Humphrey's Library, above the Divinity School, was refounded as the Bodleian: see note 211.

198 Hugh Price (or ap Rhys), a Welshman and a Doctor of Canon Law, was the prime mover in the foundation of Jesus College, Oxford, and was also the first benefactor of the College. Officially, however, the foundress was Queen Elizabeth herself.

199 Thomas Thornton, Canon of Christ Church, was Vice-Chancellor for the second time from July 1599 to July 1600. His accounts for this year of office include the sum of 50 shillings spent on the entertainment of three barons of Bohemia and others. Unfortunately no precise date is given for this entertainment and he gives no name to his guests, but it is probable that the entry refers to Waldstein and his party, and that the Windischgraetzes were assumed to be his compatriots.

The Divinity School, begun about 1420 and vaulted about 1483, probably by William Orchard, who was also in charge of Magdalen College. Sir Robert Wilbraham, in his Journal in September 1603, noted: 'The chiefest wonder in Oxford is a faire Divinitie Schoole with church windoes'. Waldstein visited it again on the 18th. (*Photo National Monuments Record*)

a very fine site, and with truly beautiful grounds. At this same time Humphrey, Duke of Gloucester, a great admirer of literature, built the Theological School which is so lovely a building that the saying of Zeuxis, '$\rho\tilde{\alpha}o\nu\ \mu\omega\mu\varepsilon\tilde{\iota}\theta\alpha\iota\ \mathring{\eta}\ \mu\iota\mu\varepsilon\tilde{\iota}\theta\alpha\iota$', could quite justifiably be inscribed above in the library which he founded.

During the reign of Henry VII Brasenose College was founded by William Smith, Bishop of Lincoln, and Corpus Christi College by Richard Fox, Bishop of Winchester.

15. Brasenose

16. Corpus Christi

Thomas Wolsey, Cardinal of York, followed these by beginning the largest and most beautiful of them all, the one which Henry VIII – incorporating Canterbury College with it – endowed with large sums of money and named Christ Church. (This Cardinal was a butcher's son, but became so rich with Church property that he subsequently laid the foundations of this college: it is so large that they had some difficulty in completing it afterwards.)

The seventeenth, Christ Church, was added to these not long ago.

In our own time Thomas Pope, knight, and Thomas Withers, a citizen of London and also a knight, re-established and provided new buildings for Durham College and St Bernard's College respectively (colleges which were then lying in ruins); they endowed them with extensive property and renamed them: the one was dedicated to St John the Baptist, the other to the Holy Trinity. Finally Hugh Price, a Doctor of Law, has – with every prospect of success – laid the foundations of a new college, Jesus, dedicated to the glory of His Name.

S̲u̲n̲d̲a̲y̲, 16 J̲u̲l̲y̲

The Vice-Chancellor of the University (the Chancellor

200 This is a mistake: the Chancellor, Thomas Sackville, Lord Buckhurst, was not Lord Admiral but Lord Treasurer.

201 Oxford had a total of six Bedels: there were three esquire Bedels, and one yeoman Bedel for each of the three Faculties of Theology, Law, and Arts (the Bedel for Arts doubled as Bedel for the Faculty of Medicine).

I have to thank Miss R. Vyse, Assistant Archivist to the Bodleian Library, for this and for much other useful information about the University.

202 He is obviously to be identified with the 'Master Leinvert, a German tailor who acts as guide to persons of our nation, and knows a good deal about the country', mentioned in the travel diary of the Duke of Stettin-Pomerania.

203 The church was the University Church of St Mary the Virgin.

The sundial had been erected by Nicolaus Kratzer in 1520 (Bodleian Library, Arch. B.C. 3, f. 76). It is noted in Anthony Wood's *Survey of the Antiquities of the City of Oxford* (1661–66, pub. Oxford Historical Society, 1889–99), but no longer exists.

> What is life? A shadow flying. Man? A vague and fleeting ray
> Which – like you, the gnomon's shadow – of a sudden fades away.
>
> These signs Time marks alway:
> The movements of the sun which goes about,
> Each changing ray,
> Each hour of day;
> The shadows on the dial shall point them out.
>
> Come boy! Why do you toss unmanly limbs in bed?
> Rise up! for slippery Time with rapid foot flies past.
> Why let the idle hours hurry by with hasty tread?
> For Time, who snatches everything, will take you too at last.
>
> 'Behold, I am Phoebus', says he: 'I measure the long year overall:
> I set; likewise do men to dust and shadows fall.'

200 is the Lord Admiral of England) came in person to visit
201 us at our lodging in a procession led by 5 Bedels, after he had read a letter in which we were given an introduction by the Cambridge Vice-Chancellor. When he had greeted us he at once asked (for we were thinking of leaving on the following day) if we needed to go so soon, and would we not first see something of the work of the University. What was more, the yearly presentations and Assemblies were due to take place within the coming week. We discussed it from every angle and at last made up our minds to stay on for at least some time, so that same evening we sent Master Linyard the tailor on ahead
202 to London with the horses.

f.165     Later the Vice-Chancellor took us to attend an Anglican service. Near the church are these verses on a
203 sundial:

> *Vita quid? Umbra fugax. Homo quid? vaga lucis imago*
> *Sic volat, ut subito gnomonis umbra cadis.*

also

> *Solis meatus lucis alternas vices*
> *Horas diurnas signa qui tempus notat*
> *Umbrae docebunt gnomonum metis suis.*

and

> *Hem puer in lecto cur mollia brachia jactas,*
> *Surge fugit celeri labilis hora pede:*
> *Cur sinas incassum celeres dilabier horas*
> *Omnia cum rapiat: te quoque tempus rapit.*

and underneath

> *En ego Phoebus ait longum qui metior annum*
> *Occido sic homines pulvis et umbra cadunt.*

After the service was over we went to Christ Church. In its very handsome kitchens there are these lines

Christ Church College

204 Two gryphons bearing pillars were the supporters of Wolsey's coat-of-arms. (This accounts for the presence of the gryphon in *Alice in Wonderland*, the author having been a Student – i.e. Fellow – of the College.) As Cardinal of York Wolsey was entitled to display the tasselled hat above his arms.

> Lo! mayest thou be proud indeed, O famous House! Allied
> To leopard and to Papal crest thou canst indeed feel pride.
> But yet, linked with the lion, be thou thrice again as proud,
> This lion has more power than the leopard is allowed.

This verse, with its reference to Wolsey's armorial leopards' heads and the cardinal's hat, is an allusion to the take-over of the College by Henry VIII. These lines are recorded in the Rawlinson MSS and they have been repainted above the chimney together with Wolsey's device, just as Waldstein describes, except that the first word is 'Esse'.

The other verses from the kitchen walls are now missing:

> Since, when it formed you, Nature made
> Merely a naked child,
> That load of poverty upon you laid –
> Bear it with patience mild.

> When she was conquered, France her flowers gave:
> England invincible, the lion brave.
> Each nation takes its emblem as its law,
> Lily or lion, when it goes to war.

These last lines, descriptive of the royal arms, were presumably inscribed below them, just as the 'Ecce superba' lines stood beneath Wolsey's. The chauvinistic implication is that in war the French are lily-livered and the English lion-hearted.

205 John Case, a scholar and Fellow of St John's, was not only a successful musician and theologian but was famous for his commentary on Aristotle, *Speculum Moralium Questionem in Universam Ethicen Aristotelis* (1585), the first book to be printed by the Oxford University Press. He had died early in 1600.

His epitaph means: 'Case lies in death, but though buried, he lives.' In the Latin there is a mild pun on the philosopher's name. The library window on which this was written must have been replaced not long afterwards, for the College Librarian informed me that this is the only record of the inscription.

206 John Rainolds (or Reynolds) had become President of Corpus Christi College in 1598. He was staunchly Puritan and was publicly rebuked by the Queen herself when she visited Oxford in 1592 'for his obstinate preciseness', but though stubborn in his opinions he appears to have been a man of the utmost integrity and kindness. He was one of the most learned scholars in the kingdom and the most eminent of those selected by James I for the Hampton Court Conference which led to the Authorized Version of the Bible.

207 Most unfortunately the Battel Book entries for the period June–September 1600 are missing, so there is no College record of Waldstein's visit.

painted, together with the device of the cardinal's hat and two gryphons:

> *Ecce superba potes domus inclyta, tum leopardo*
> *Pontificisque armis esse superba potes.*
> *Sed tamen a triplici magis esto superba leone*
> *Hic leo plus juris quam leopardus habet.*

also

> *Infantem nudum cum te natura creavit*
> *Paupertatis onus patienter ferre memento.*

and

> *Gallia victa dedit flores, invicta leonem*
> *Anglia, jus belli in flore leone suum.*

Next we visited St John's College; its library has a window inscribed with:

> *Casus in occasum tendit vivitque sepultus*

a line referring to the well-known philosopher John Case, a Fellow of this College.

We were invited to dinner at the Vice-Chancellor's; the erudite and celebrated Rainolds was also present.

MONDAY, 17 JULY
Had lunch in Christ Church as guests of one of the Doctoral Candidates who greeted us as 'most noble kings'. There too we were splendidly entertained: not only was it a sumptuous meal, but, with the extreme courtesy which the English show, they invited us to lead the procession.

TUESDAY, 18 JULY
Visited Magdalen College, famous for its long and beautiful walk and for its unusually large grounds (it

*Mary Magdalen's*

208 That is, 80 yards (73 m) across the College grounds from the gate in the High to the original main gate of the quadrangle. The distance is slightly exaggerated.

209 Waldstein saw the doorknocker shaped like a grotesque nose which is now affixed to the top of the College gate. What was probably the original Brazen Nose from which the College took its name, a Romanesque sanctuary knocker of lion mask type, had been carried off to Stamford by schismatic students in 1333 and was repurchased only in 1890. It is now in the hall.

210 The Divinity School was complete by 1490. Except for the addition of a doorway by Sir Christopher Wren (so that processions could pass straight into the Sheldonian), the room retains its original appearance.

The Moderator's chair remained in its place at the west end of the building until the middle of the nineteenth century.

211 Duke Humphrey's Library is directly above, rather than 'adjoining', the Divinity School, and contemporary with it. The collection presented by Humphrey, Duke of Gloucester, had been despoiled by the violently Protestant Commission of Edward VI: the most obviously Papist books had been destroyed, and the remainder left to decay or be stolen. Finally the bookcases were sold. Thomas Bodley, recently returned from diplomatic service abroad, had made his historic offer to restore the library at his own cost only three years before Waldstein's visit.

The coats-of-arms are those of Bodley and of the University. Describing the latter, Waldstein has miscopied his notes: the book, representing the one referred to in Revelation, has not two but seven seals.

It may be true that Bodley had some buyers abroad, but he acquired most of the books by pertinacious soliciting of his friends and acquaintances. Among the gifts which he lists in a letter to the Vice-Chancellor on 25 June 1600, only a few weeks before Waldstein saw the library, is 'my L. of Essex gift, about Three hundred volumes of wch the far greater part are Bookes in folio' – i.e. loot from the library of Bishop Osorio (see note 169). (A copy of Bodley's letter is in the Register of Convocation for the period.)

212 Gentilis was Regius Professor of Civil Law. He fully deserves Waldstein's description of 'very distinguished', for he founded the science of international law and was the first jurist to make law independent of theological differences. He had reached England in 1580, a Protestant fugitive from Ancona. At Oxford he quickly made such a reputation that within a few years he was consulted as to the proper course to be taken with the Spanish Ambassador, who in 1584 was discovered to be plotting against the Queen.

stands 80 yards from its gates). Next we went to the College of the Brazen Nose: it is this, attached to the College gates, which gives the place its name. From here we went to the Divinity School, which is extremely fine; it contains a high professorial chair made of stone. Adjoining it there is a very beautiful library, the ceiling decorated with coats-of-arms and devices. Here the arms of the University are displayed: 3 crowns, a book with 2 seals, and the inscription 'Dominus illuminatio mea'. It has identical bookshelves on either side and two study-rooms. It was built by a private citizen of Oxford, Thomas Bodley; at his own expense he employs people in different parts of Europe and they collect choice books for the library here.

Divinity School

Since we had now made up our minds to wait for the day of the Oxford Assemblies, we went this evening to another lodging, a private hostel kept by a good fellow called Sherburn, and remained there, living on our own provisions, for the best part of a week.

WEDNESDAY, 19 JULY
Went this morning to Lincoln College. In the evening after dinner we went back to this college – it being in the same part of the town as our hostel – and listened to some very learned declamations and to the disputations they provoked.

THURSDAY, 20 JULY
This evening a very distinguished Italian, the Oxford Professor Alberic Gentilis, called on us; we then went out with him and enjoyed ourselves on a boating trip.

# OXFORD

*A map of the city, c. 1650. North is at the bottom. From the bottom right a very broad street, St Giles's, leads up to the city walls; its line narrows and crosses the city to the top (south), where the vast quadrangle of Christ Church stands just inside the walls. At the right (west) end of the city is the Castle, from which a long west-east road runs to the bridge and Magdalen College, outside the walls. East of its junction with the north-south axis (at Carfax) this is the High Street, marked halfway along by the large, spired church of St Mary the Virgin. Below and to the right of this church is Lincoln College, near which Waldstein stayed; above it to the left, inside the walls, is Merton. (British Museum, London)*

*The cup of buffalo horn in fourteenth-century silver-gilt mounts presented to the Queen's College, Oxford, by its founder. A few details, such as the eagle finial, are seventeenth-century. (Reproduced by permission of the Queen's College)*

*'A very beautiful library, the ceiling decorated with coats-of-arms and devices. . . . It has identical bookshelves on either side': Duke Humphrey's Library, the oldest part of the Bodleian, newly fitted out in Waldstein's day. (Photo Edwin Smith)*

213 The collection, a particularly fine one, is still in the possession of All Souls.

214 The gift of Robert Eglesfield, who founded the College in the name of Queen Philippa, consort of Edward III, the cup is among the greatest treasures of the Queen's College.

215 The effigies of Thomas Pope and of his wife (herself a benefactress of the College) are very fine ones: they can still be seen in Trinity College Chapel, having been preserved when the chapel which Waldstein saw was rebuilt towards the end of the seventeenth century.

216 Merton College Library had been only recently completed when Waldstein saw it, and is still almost precisely the same as it was at that date. The 'two departments' are the lines of bays, one on each side of the room. (A second room, very similar in design, was added in the 1620s.)

    The book was the *Catalogus Vetus* (Old Catalogue), which no longer exists. A sixteenth-century copy of it known as the Savile Catalogue is in the College Library, and the two extracts quoted appear there with only very slightly different wording:

    'John Duns Hilpret Scotus, a man of great and discriminating mind: because of his perspicacity his wisdom as a Doctor was proclaimed by the Pope: he committed to writing a huge and varied body of work. He lived in the reign of Edward II.'

    'And in the reign of Edward III lived that expert philosopher and distinguished theologian John Wycliffe, Rector of Loughborough; wise and prudent as an upholder of the pure truth of the Gospel, he had an eminent and clearly inspired power of mind against the hypocrisy and blindness of his own age. He was the author of an immense and almost incalculable number of philosophical and theological works.'

    The connection of Duns Scotus with Merton is generally considered non-proven, but Wycliffe's Fellowship is attested by a bursarial roll of 1356 in which he is listed as one of the Fellows who did duty as steward at the Fellows' table.

    I have to thank Mr J. Burgass of Merton College Library for this information.

217 One of the subjects which Congregation proposed for incepting M.A.s upon this occasion was the (presumably Shakespeare-inspired) question: 'an uxor perversa humanitate potius quam asperitate sanetur?', i.e. 'whether a shrewish wife may be better cured by kindness than by severity?'. It is recorded that the question was answered in the affirmative. (See A. Clark, *Register of the University of Oxford, 1571–1622*, Oxford, 1885 etc.)

218 Dr Thomas Holland was Regius Professor of Divinity 1589–1611.

219 The Diary has 'de Peregrinatione'. The word might perhaps mean simply 'pilgrimage', but this seems an unprofitable subject for 'some really good declamations', and the Rev. R. E. Gleed, Rector of Avening, suggested to me a much more probably interpretation of the word: the practice – followed in Roman Catholic countries on the Feast of Corpus Christi – of making a procession through the streets with the consecrated Host displayed in a monstrance. Such processions had been strongly condemned in the original Articles of Belief and in the Articles of 1571: 'The Sacrament of the Lordes Supper was not by Christes ordinaunce reserved, caryed about, lyfted up, or worshipped.'

## Friday, 21 July

Went to All Souls' College where there is a collection of annotated manuscripts, and then to the Queen's College which has a cup made from a horn and decorated with silver-gilt rings. After this to Trinity College: here they have the alabaster tomb of Thomas Pope, knight, the founder of this College, together with that of his wife. We also visited Merton College: there are two departments in its library, one is for manuscripts only, the other for printed books. They have a book containing the names of all the Fellows of the College with the kings of England under whose reigns they lived. What is written about John Scotus and Wycliffe is of particular interest:

> *Joannes Duns Hilpret Scotus vir magni et subtilis ingenii Doctor subtilis est declaratus per Papam suae subtilitatis immensa monumenta et ab multa scriptis mandavit. Vixit rege 2 Eduardo.*
>
> *Et 3 Eduardo primus fuit Joannes Wiklef exercitatissimus Philosophus, et clarissimus Theologus: Rector Lutterbortensis cordatissimus assertor Evangelicae puritatis, contra sui soeculi hÿpocritas et tenebriones excellentis et plane divini ingenii, immensa et pene innumera monumenta Philosophica et Theologica conscripsit.*

## Saturday, 22 July

The Commencement of the Oxford Assemblies. Some excellent lectures were given during the morning by various Professors: we ourselves attended a lecture in Theology given by an extremely learned man named Holland. In the afternoon the Theological disputations took place. There were some really good declamations on the subject of Peregrination.

The Windischgraetzes joined us, and in the evening we took out a boat and enjoyed some music.

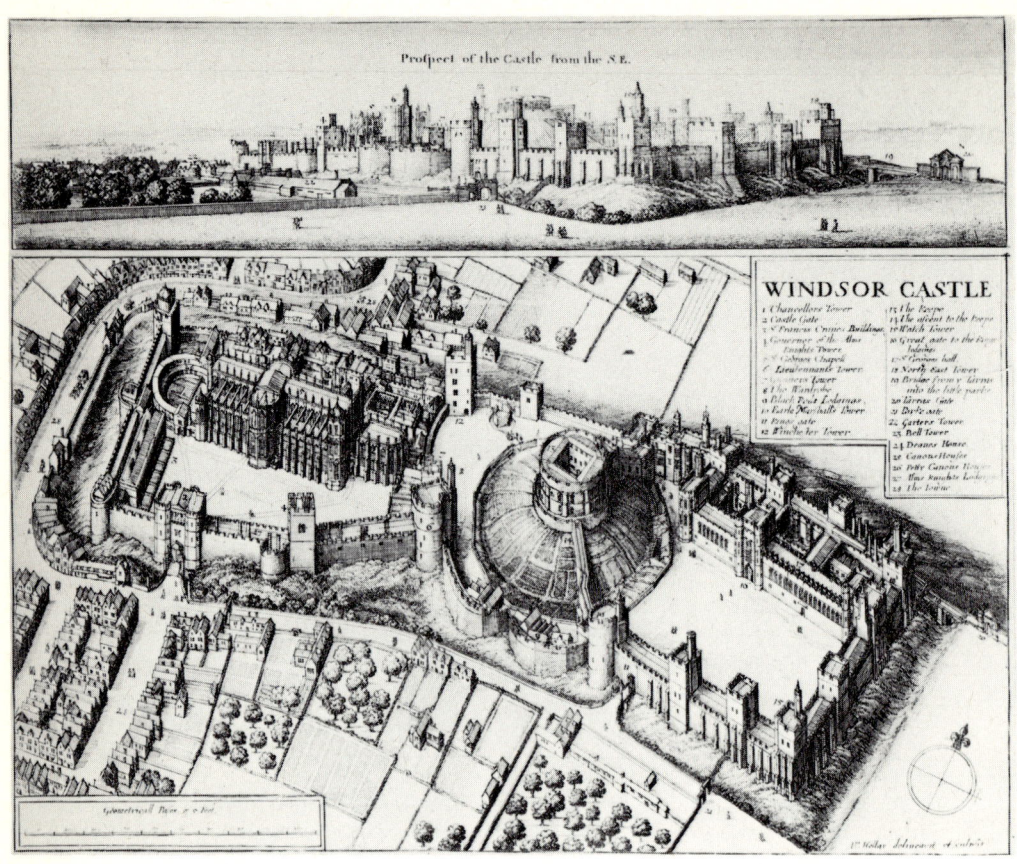

Windsor Castle seen from the south-east, and in bird's eye view. St George's Chapel is on the far side of the left-hand courtyard. The Royal Apartments surround the right-hand court, and were entered by a large gate in the middle of the far side. To the right of that gate is St George's Hall. The Round Tower crowns the motte in the centre. (Engraving by Hollar, 1647. British Museum, London)

Sunday, 23 July
Lunched in Magdalen College. After going for a trip on the river we spent the evening with the Windischgraetzes.

Monday, 24 July
Another day of Assemblies, also the actual conferring of degrees, first the Masters and then the Doctors. In the evening we presented ourselves at Christ Church for the Doctoral dinner to which we had been invited.

Soon after midnight and by the light of the moon (it was quite impossible to ride by day as the weather was so unbearably hot) we left Oxford with the Windischgraetzes.

Tuesday, 25 July
By 7 o'clock this morning we had done 20 miles and had reached the town of Wycombe where we rested for an hour or two and had some breakfast; then, 10 miles beyond Wycombe we came to Windsor Castle in the county of Berkshire.

*The Palace of Windsor*

This palace is particularly famous for the beauty of its situation, and (to use Camden's description) 'Calmly from its hill-top it enjoys the most delightful view in the world. It gazes down over the prospect of a wide and far-reaching vale, patterned with ploughland, green with its meadows, clad here and there with woodlands, and watered by the softly flowing Thames. Behind it the hills rise all around, neither rough nor very high, but crowned with woods as though Nature herself had dedicated them to the chase. Kings, impressed with its beauty, have very often made it their residence, and here the mighty King

220 Eton and King's were founded by Henry VI in 1440–41; the connection between them was made three years later and is still maintained.

Eton College Chapel had been intended as the choir of an immense church, never completed on account of the Wars of the Roses.

Edward III, conqueror of France, was born. It was he who rebuilt the present castle so that it almost rivals a town, gave it tremendous fortifications of squared masonry with fosses and ramparts, and immediately afterwards – since he had subdued both France and Scotland – he imprisoned here at one and the same time John the King of France and David King of Scotland.'

Before going into the castle we first visited a college which has a magnificent church attached to it: we were told that this was a place which prepared scholars for King's College, Cambridge.

Next they went into the castle itself. There are three separate courtyards: in the first of them is the church (of which more later). The second courtyard, like the first, is enclosed by a wall, and in the middle of it there is a round tower standing on quite a high mound ringed with double walls and ditches. Then comes a third courtyard encircled by splendid palace buildings; it looks a worthy dwelling-place for the Queen's Majesty. Here there is a raised basin or fountain-head of marble, and the water, we were told, is brought by pipes from 5 miles away.

By mounting some steps from this courtyard into the Royal Apartments themselves, you can see a room in which there were 5 beds, gilded and majestically rich, and spread with priceless coverlets; one of them was 12 feet wide and is said to have been Henry VIII's; another belonged to Anne Boleyn, mother of the Queen Elizabeth now on the throne; another was Henry VIII's and Edward VI's. There are two Turkish bows in the room and also a most beautifully made marble table. Hanging on the wall here is a French tapestry showing

221 The best description of this tapestry is in Platter's diary: 'a very ancient arras stretched against the wall, worked in silk and gold, which the English took from the French. The story worked on it tells how the three lilies fell from heaven out of an angel's hand into the hut of the hermit of Remigi who was holding a chaplet, and he gave them to King Clovis' consort and instructed her in the Christian faith so that she became a Christian, and he advised her to hand the three lilies to her lord the king and persuade him likewise to become a Christian, so that he should be the first Christian sovereign, and to bear these three lilies as arms, instead of the three toads he had previously borne, as it came to pass, and the French still bear the lilies for their emblem today.'

Platter adds that the French had often tried to buy this tapestry back, offering very large sums for it, 'but it is not to be purchased from England at any price'.

In the Musée St Rémi at Rheims there is a tapestry of the Battle of Tolbiac which depicts the story: Clovis is fighting in a yellow surcoat charged with three black toads; an inset shows his baptism and the angel handing down the lilies of France.

222 This was the famous unicorn's horn referred to in Henry Peacham's limping hexameter (see note 85). It was probably a narwhal's horn.

223 Other writers mentioned this bird of paradise, and W. B. Rye (*England as seen by Foreigners in the Days of Elizabeth and James I*, London, 1865) suspected that it was an ornithological fraud: 'The high value set upon these birds, whose plumes were worn in the turbans of Oriental chiefs, awakened the cupidity and trickery of the Chinese, who manufactured from parrots, parrakeets and other gay specimens of the feathered tribes, *artificial* Birds of Paradise.'

The two fairly detailed descriptions of the bird (Hentzner's and Platter's) do not tally precisely, but they agree that it was three spans in length, partially yellow, and that it had, as Hentzner puts it, 'two fibres or nerves, bigger at their ends, but like a pretty strong thread of a leaden colour inclining to black, with which, as it has no feet, it is said to fasten itself to trees when it wants to rest'. These 'fibres or nerves' are characteristic of certain types of bird of paradise, and the Curator of Birds at the London Zoo told me that although he could not make a positive identification from the descriptions, they agreed far too closely with known species for there to be any likelihood of fraud.

The odd belief that birds of paradise were legless was derived from the fact that Oriental taxidermists used to cut off the legs of the birds which they preserved. The Latin name of the greater bird of paradise is still *Paradisea apoda*, i.e. 'without feet'.

224 St George's Hall has been reconstructed since Waldstein's visit, but its appearance at the time can be seen in an etching by Hollar, published in Elias Ashmole's *Institution . . . of the Most Noble Order of the Garter* (1672; facsimile, London, 1971).

225 'The companion of industry is its reward; All wisdom is from God; Wisdom is the ruler of Nature.'

Eisenberg supplies the fourth inscription which Waldstein omits. It was 'Virtutis laus actio', a more epigrammatic form of Cicero's 'Virtutis laus omnis in actione consistit', i.e. 'The whole glory of virtue is in action'.

226 This is true now, and was evidently so then even though the Round Tower was 30 feet (9 m) lower than it is at present. Its height was raised when George IV had it repaired and partially rebuilt.

227 Not strictly accurate, though it is doubtless what visitors have often been told. David II, King of Scotland, and John, King of France, were imprisoned at Windsor Castle by Edward III after the battles of Neville's Cross (1346) and Poitiers (1356) respectively. They were not lodged in the Round Tower, however: their rooms are believed to have been in the so-called 'Norman Gateway' at the entrance to the Upper Ward of the Castle.

the King of France, an angel, and the three lilies of the French royal arms. The room also contains the present Queen Elizabeth's bed, a horn which is 9 spans long, and a bird of paradise. There is a beautifully embroidered cushion done by Queen Elizabeth herself in red and white silk.

After this you pass through a number of rooms hung with various tapestries, and then you come to a most magnificent chapel: the roof is vaulted and is made most sumptuously of gilded wood. An interesting thing here is the chair used by the Queen when she attends services. The hall called St George's Hall is close by, and there the Knights of the Garter assemble.

In another room there is a picture of a naval battle fought by Henry V; it was in this same room that Edward VI was born. Next, in one of the Queen's own apartments, there is a table made entirely of coral of different colours. It has an inscription around its four sides:

*Industriae comes praemium: omnis sapientia a Deo: regina rerum sapientia.*

After this comes a fairly long upper walk or gallery. This contains the Queen's couch where she sits when she wishes to consult privately with her ministers. A little lower down is a very fine gallery with a glorious view of the hills, the valleys, the woods, and the meadows all around.

We then climbed the tower, which is in the centre of the second courtyard. Its roof is covered with lead, and from it you can see the tower of St Paul's in London. It was in this tower that the two Kings, of France and of Scotland, were kept prisoner.

# WINDSOR CASTLE

228 Waldstein, who has already acknowledged Camden as the source of his description of Windsor, now quotes him again for the account of the Order of the Garter. Camden himself used Stow's *Of the Castell of Wyndsore* as his own main source (British Library, Harl. MS 367, ff. 13r, 13v).

229 Despite the popular and charming (but not at all contemporary) story about the King and the Countess of Salisbury, Edward III's choice of the Garter as the symbol of the highest honour has never been conclusively explained. The reason given by Waldstein is as likely as any.

230 This claim is now discounted.
I am indebted to Miss G. Holmes, Custodian of the Muniments, and to Mr R. Mackworth-Young, Librarian of Windsor Castle, for supplying me with much interesting information about Windsor.

231 This is inaccurate. Since 1519 stall plates have been fixed within a year of a Garter Knight's installation, and not after his death.

232 Their helmets, crests, and mantlings were also displayed, as they still are.

233 The present canopy over the Sovereign's stall is eighteenth-century work; the stall itself dates from about 1480.

*Details from a symbolic picture of the Garter Procession in 1576. From left to right are Queen Elizabeth, a nobleman carrying the Sword of State, and Philip II of Spain and Henry III of France. Windsor Castle appears in the background, though the procession would have taken place within it. (Engravings by Marcus Gheeraerts. British Museum, London)*

After this you come to a very stately church dedicated to the Virgin Mary and to St George of Cappadocia by Edward III; it was Edward IV, however, who gave the building its magnificent appearance. Here Edward III, in order to honour military valour with glory, reward, and splendour, enrolled the Most Noble Companionship of Golden Knights, and to these – because of his own garter which had been given him as a symbol of a battle which he had successfully fought – he gave the name 'Equites Periscilidis' or 'Knights of the Garter'. These Knights wear a blue garter round the left leg with a French inscription on it in gold: HONI SOIT QUI MAL Y PENSE. Some people, however, attribute the founding of the Order to Richard the First.

In any case, a number of the most powerful monarchs of the Christian world have belonged to this Companionship and have worn this symbol of the highest honour. From the time when the Order, which consists of 26 Knights, was first established, some 20 kings already (excluding kings of England who are Sovereigns of the Order) have been invested, the following among them: the Emperors Charles V and Maximilian, and the Kings Henry III and IV of France, Frederick of Denmark, and Philip of Spain. Knights who have died have their names placed upon the walls on bronze tablets inscribed with their rank. The standards and swords of living Knights hang from above; on a raised dais there is a stall which, as well as its standard and sword, has the royal arms of England carved in wood on its canopy: here the Sovereign of the Order sits. We saw the ceremonial dress used for the investiture of Knights, i.e. a mantle with a scarlet collar.

*Notable church at Windsor*

*Origin of the Golden Knights*

234  It was Jane Seymour's grave, not Anne Boleyn's, which (in accordance with the terms of the King's will) was opened to receive Henry VIII's body.

235  The monument stood in what is now the Albert Memorial Chapel. Wolsey had commissioned Benedetto da Rovezzano to construct his tomb; after Wolsey's fall Henry VIII decided that it should be used for himself, but with the following alterations: the whole tomb was to be mounted on a large marble plinth with a bronze frieze; a set of massive bronze candlesticks was to be added; Henry's own effigy, his royal arms, and other insignia were to be substituted for Wolsey's, and the original four corner pillars which supported angels were to be replaced by a series of at least eight pillars 10 feet (3 m) high, surmounted by Apostles and with standing figures at their bases.

Some of this work was carried out, as Waldstein's description indicates, but it was still uncompleted at the time of Henry's death and the tomb was never used for him. In Commonwealth times the metal, including the effigy of the King, was stripped off and sold (Millar, *Inventories*). The two great candlesticks in St George's Chapel are modern copies of the originals, which went to St Bavon's Cathedral in Ghent. The marble sarcophagus remained in the Chapel until it and the base on which it rested were used for Nelson's tomb in the crypt of St Paul's Cathedral.

Hampton Court Palace from the river. The tallest building is the hall with its great roof, in the centre; on the left is the Main Gate (now much lower), in the centre the now-vanished Royal Apartments. (From a painting by an unknown artist, c. 1640. Reproduced by gracious permission of Her Majesty The Queen)

*f.170*     For the rest, this church both inside and out is as choice and splendid as any in England. It is particularly striking for its profusion of beautifully worked stone pendants hanging in the English style; the roof is raised high upon arches and is lavishly surfaced with lead.

    There is an epitaph to Edward IV and his queen here; Henry VIII and Anne Boleyn are buried in the centre of the choir, but there is no monument to them, only a cloth laid over their tomb. One can still see, in another part of this church, the monument – relatively new and of the superbest workmanship – which Thomas Wolsey ordered to be made for his own tomb; this, however, as well as all the rest of his property, became forfeit to the Crown after his impeachment for treason. It is oval in form and made of cast bronze with 7 columns rising in a circle, two of which are surmounted by pairs of gilt angels; there are 4 larger and 4 smaller statues set between the columns themselves. In the centre is the effigy upon 4 pillars of equal height, and between these pillars is the tomb itself where the body lies: this receptacle for the coffin is of black and white marble. One single wing of these gilt angels is so heavy that a man can barely lift it off the ground. The royal arms of England are also here, cast in bronze.

    After leaving the castle we hurried along the 4 miles to the town of Staines. This is a very charming place right beside the river. We put up here for the night.

## WEDNESDAY, 26 JULY

Made an early start, and after crossing the bridge and going 6 miles along a most picturesque road, we arrived at Hampton Court.

*Royal palace of Hampton Court*

236 This was the general opinion, and most descriptions of Hampton Court Palace at this period bubble over with superlatives. Thage Thott, who accompanied King Christian IV of Denmark on his state visit to James I in 1606, wrote: 'When the meal was over, they [the two Kings] went on to the castle of Hampton Court which is the finest palace in the whole of England. The rooms and apartments are hung full of fine tapestries most beautifully worked in silk and gold; they cannot, I believe, be equalled anywhere.' (My thanks to the Royal Library, Copenhagen, for permission to quote from Thott's manuscript Diary.)

Jacob Rathgeb, in the Duke of Württemberg's Diary (1592), expressed the same opinion even more vigorously: 'This is the most splendid and most magnificent royal palace of any that may be found in England or indeed in any other kingdom ... all the apartments and rooms in this immensely large structure are hung with rich tapestry, of pure gold and fine silk, so exceedingly beautiful and royally ornamented that it would hardly be possible to find more magnificent things of the kind in any other place.'

237 Waldstein inadvertently left the bracket open.

238 In 1521 Giovanni da Maiano made a set of eight terracotta roundels of the early Roman Emperors for the Clock Court of Wolsey's palace at Hampton. These roundels were originally coloured and gilded, and a similar set was made for the splendid Holbein Gate at Whitehall. The royal arms and the busts on the Main Gate at Hampton Court are of the same date.

239 This was the fountain 'artistically wrought of white marble' (Platter) which Rathgeb describes as follows: 'In the middle of the first and principal court stands a splendid high and massy fountain with an ingenious water work by which you can, if you like, make the water play upon the ladies and others who are standing by, and give them a thorough wetting.'

240 Platter explains in much greater detail: 'all manner of shapes, men and women, half men and half horse, sirens, serving maids with baskets, French lilies, and delicate crenellations, all made from dry twigs bound together and the aforesaid quickset shrubs [he has just mentioned hedges of juniper, holly, box, etc.] or entirely of rosemary, all true to the life, and so clearly and amusingly interwoven ... that their equal would be difficult to find.'

241 There is no reference to timber from Ireland in the builders' accounts; these mention oak, chiefly from the great forested areas which then existed in neighbouring Surrey. (My thanks to the Inspectorate of Ancient Buildings, Department of the Environment, for the information.) Zinzerling, however, makes the same statement about the roof of the Great Hall, so it is clearly the information given to visitors.

242 'Long live Queen Elizabeth, in whom is the source of all wise dealing.'

The Royal Apartments described by Waldstein were destroyed in the late seventeenth century to make way for Wren's rebuilding.

This palace is situated by the Thames on a very long and wide alluvial plain: it is larger than any other in England so it is commonly – and deservedly – known as 'England's Wateringplace'. This is considered to be the most splendid of the palaces and to be the best for its collection of tapestries. The view one gets from the palace is quite equally profitable and lovely, with its abundant and very extensive parkland (as much as 3 miles of it, walled in the whole way round.

On entering the palace gate you come to a courtyard with buildings on all sides. On the gateway are busts of Trajan and Hadrian; also the Queen's arms with the usual motto 'Dieu et mon Droict'. We went through another gateway into a fine quadrangle which has some really splendid buildings on the far side of it; on one side of this gate are the busts of Tiberius, Julius Caesar, and the Emperor Vitellius. This quadrangle is paved with squared stone and in the centre there is a fountain with a golden crown around the top of it: above this stands a gilt figure of Justice. This fountain spurts its water out of marble columns.

Next we went into the garden. This is especially interesting because of its many avenues and also for the large number of growing plants shaped into animals, in fact they even had sirens, centaurs, sphinxes, and other fabulous poetic creatures portrayed here in topiary work.

Going up into the left wing of the palace one comes to an enormous hall with an arched roof made of some Irish wood which, so they say, has the natural property of keeping free from cobwebs. In another room there is a fireplace with the inscription 'Vivat regina Elisabetha, in qua fons omnis prudentiae'. We then entered a room

*The palace gateway*

*The garden*

*Rooms*

243 Platter makes the same comment on this set of tapestries: 'The history of Pompey was embroidered after the life.' I suspect that we are listening to the guide.
  Tapestries were of the very greatest value; three of the sets mentioned were valued by Cromwell's assessors in 1649 (Millar, *Inventories*):

| | |
|---|---|
| Tenn peeces of Rich Arras of ye history of Julius Caesar | £5,022 |
| Tenn peeces of Arras Hangings of ye storye of Abraham | £8,260 |
| Nyne peeces of Arras, of ye story of Tobias | £3,409 |

244 This bed is described in great detail in Cromwell's Inventories: 'One Bedstedd apparrelled with rich crimson cloth of gould Tissue enbroydered with K. Henry ye 8t his Lres Crowned &c cont Ceeler, Tester, Vallances and bases all of the same stuffe, The Armes of England richly Enbroydered on the Ceeler & Tester.' The description continues, and includes the five bed curtains which were 'of Orringe, cullored cloth of gould', four side curtains and also foot curtains, laced with broad gold lace and garnished with buttons. (Millar, *Inventories*.)

The Great Hall of Hampton Court Palace, built in 1531–36. The tapestries hanging on the walls are part of the famous Abraham series, woven in Brussels c. 1540 and purchased by Henry VIII. They were not sold at the Commonwealth, but retained by Cromwell for his own use. (Photo Department of the Environment, Crown Copyright reserved)

which had the whole of its ceiling gilt. A vast gallery leads out of it and the ceiling of this is gilded also.

After this we saw the Queen's chapel: it has a heavily gilded roof and contains a splendid organ; ten gilt angels support the massive weight of the vaulted wooden roof. Coming down to the lower chapel, which is just as magnificent in every way as the upper one, you see on the door: 'Vivat Elisabetha Regina, ANNO 1570'. In this chapel 45 urns are hanging, with numerous names inscribed on them in gold lettering.

One of the next rooms has a picture showing two monks and the Crucifixion. Also, in one special room, there is a most beautiful picture of the Night of Christ's Passion and the Last Supper of Our Saviour, painted with such skill that if the windows are closed and the red curtains of the room drawn, the picture gives the impression of being real, and succeeds most wonderfully in representing the effects of night time.

*Cleverly painted picture of the Passion*

We went into one room decorated with very large and choice tapestries showing the story of Julius Caesar and Pompey. Best of all is the one of Pompey's murder on the coast of Egypt: the picture is woven into the tapestry to the very life. In a further – and heavily gilded – room called the Presence Chamber one can see fabulously rich hangings, in another the most sumptuous beds such as Henry VIII's, which is most gorgeously decorated with gold and is said to have been used on his expedition to Boulogne; there is another bed here, gilt all over, which also belonged to Henry VIII, and in this bed his Queen gave birth to Edward VI. Still another bed has silk-covered cushions and hangings which really are majestic: very richly woven in gold.

245 This, as Waldstein's description implies, was the *pièce de résistance* of the whole Palace, and it finds its way into almost every contemporary account. Zinzerling sums it up: 'it captivates the eyes of all who enter'. (He then complains that he had to haggle with the guide about the amount of the latter's fee for showing him round.)

246 This was an extremely large square diamond, which Platter tells us was 'worth many thousands of crowns'.

247 Platter puts a price on this also, writing that this table-covering, 'red and inset with precious stones and pearls, is valued at over 50,000 crowns. Not do I ever remember seeing larger or finer pearls before.'

248 The spelling he uses is 'Leberfoliz', just as it sounded to his ears. Since 'Labour's Follies' was a game, and the connection of ideas between Labour and Love was then so strong, it is probable that Shakespeare, who needed a Euphuistic title for a lovers' comedy, had this game in mind when he picked on *Love's Labour's Lost*; he subsequently followed it up with the missing (or perhaps alternatively titled) *Love's Labour's Won*.

The rich Canopy of State at Hampton Court, like the Paradise Chamber itself, no longer exists, but some idea of it may be had from this painting showing Henry VIII seated under another embroidered canopy bearing the royal arms. (Detail of a painting by an unknown artist representing the King at Whitehall; see also colour plate I. Reproduced by gracious permission of Her Majesty The Queen)

There is another room with the most beautiful tapestries, depicting the stories of Abraham, of Melchizedek, and of Tobias. And then comes that far-famed and simply overwhelming room of quite unimaginable riches – the 'Paradise Chamber', so named for its truly vast profusion of different gems of fabulous value. Quite especially notable is the Canopy of State, made to the order of Henry VIII, which stands above the throne. In this canopy are the royal arms of England in gold, encircled by the Garter and studded with pearls of stupendously huge size: particularly memorable is the diamond hanging from the extreme end of the Garter. This diamond is reckoned to be worth 500 English pounds. Another really marvellous thing is a cloth for a table, embroidered all over with pearls and almost too heavy to lift; in addition to this there is a large number of cushions, every one of which is embroidered with pearls and precious stones. Underneath the canopy stands the throne: this is in every way as gorgeous as the canopy itself. The same room contains a dicing game made of silver and wood which they call 'Labour's Follies', a mother-of-pearl table and a cushion on it covered all over with pearls, a jewelled water-clock, a fine looking-glass decorated with pearls, a chess set made of alabaster, the ivory flutes which are used by the Queen's musicians, and a picture of Henry VIII. Finally there is the roof of this room: it is most beautifully decorated with astronomical figures, and in one part of it there is a picture of the Queen being received into Heaven.

From here one goes into a kind of gallery where there is a splendid looking-glass done in gold, also an alabaster

*[margin notes: Very beautiful PARADISE Chamber; Canopy; Table cloth]*

249 This is a guess, and not a very satisfactory one. As with 'Labour's Follies' he writes down the English word by ear, but unfortunately the first letter is illegible. His word is '?ecome'. Ordinary coal was then known as sea-coal (it came to London from Newcastle by boat), in contradistinction to charcoal which was locally produced, but coal, though mined, is not a metal, nor does it seem to have a notably 'extraordinary name'. It is difficult however to think of any other substance at all likely to have been put into the stove.

250 'Having lost my chastity I cannot go on living.'

251 Eisenberg refers to this as 'The picture of Venus as a lovely young lady' and adds that underneath was written 'In hac poesi figurantur proprietates Amoris' – 'The characteristics of Love are here poetically depicted.' The inscriptions mean: 'The Representation of Love', 'Far and Near', 'Death and Life', and 'Winter and Summer'.

252 Hero of Roman legend: when a deep chasm opened in the Forum, seers declared that it would never close unless Rome's most precious possession were to be thrown into it. Realizing that nothing was of such value to the city as a brave citizen, Marcus Curtius mounted his horse and rode fully armed over the edge of the gulf which at once closed above him.

249 thurible for burning incense. In the Queen's bathroom there is a stove, and in its upper part is a certain metal which the English call by the extraordinary name of 'sea-coal'; by heating this the room itself is warmed. We saw too the story of Christ's Passion cut in mother-of-pearl.

f.173 In another such gallery there is an engraving on copper of the city of Antwerp; a very large looking-glass with the inscription 'Salvator Mundi'; and pictures of the Emperor Charles V, of Mary Stuart Queen of Scotland, of Tarquin and Lucretia with the inscription 'Amissa
250 pudicitia superstes esse nequeo', and of Love, represented as a virgin: above her head is written 'Imago Amoris', on her forehead 'Procul et Prope', on her breast 'Mors et
251 Vita', at her feet 'Hyems et Aestas'. There is a bust in
252 bronze of Marcus Curtius; a picture in which a king is shown sitting in judgment, with the inscription 'The truly wise king will keep one ear for the defendant, knowing well that the accused often has a better case than his accuser'; and a figure of Obedience with the words 'Obedience is the best of all the virtues'. In addition there is a whole quantity of chairs, each one of them upholstered in materials woven of silk and gold. Another room contains very large furnishings of regal splendour – coverlets for beds and also decorative covers for chairs and tables.

Among other things that we saw was the state mantle of Edward the Sixth, the Ireland mantle, and also a robe of white linen, beautifully embroidered with white silk, which we were told was worn by Edward the Sixth at his christening.

After this we visited the Royal Library: over the door stands a white marble bust of Edward VI. The library

*The Royal Library*

253 This is probably to be identified with 'A Cupp of Unicorn's horne richly garnish't with gold', referred to in Cromwell's Inventories (Millar, *Inventories*.)

254 Platter, more sceptically, describes this as being 'silver-gilt'.

255
        Whoso is asked, I tell you, sing:
        'May Elizabeth live for ever'.

256
        Phoebus be present; and when Her Grace's finger strikes the keys
        Make the tinkling strings resound with tuneful melodies.

257 The word *Kamfoeder* is still in use in some Germanic languages; it means precisely what Waldstein says, 'a receptacle for combs', but it was also applied to all kinds of dressing case, including very elaborate ones. I have found no other reference to one 'shaped like a man'.

258 Built by Henry VIII. As soon as he acquired the site, near Kingston in Surrey, he renamed it Nonsuch, intending from the first that it should be, as indeed it was, a palace without rival. A village was destroyed to make way for it, and work began in 1538.

    The palace survived Cromwell's regime but was given by Charles II to his mistress, Barbara Villiers, Duchess of Cleveland, who sold it for demolition to the Earl of Berkeley. Dismantling had begun by 1683; much of the material went to the rebuilding of Durdans, Berkeley's residence at Epsom. The site was excavated in 1959. (See J. Dent, *The Quest for Nonsuch*, rev. ed., London, 1970.)

    Waldstein's opening paragraph describing Nonsuch (from 'This is a place' to 'unity with Health') is taken word for word from Camden's *Britannia*. Waldstein has omitted only the original name of the place (Cuddington) and the name of the poet whose Latin verses are quoted (Leland).

has a good variety of books and also houses a number of choice royal possessions. These include a walking-stick made from a unicorn's horn, other sticks containing watches, Henry VIII's skull-cap embroidered with gold wire and of considerable weight, an elk's horn, a horn cup which is said to break in pieces if you put poison in it, cases standing on the floor full of gilt glasses, a horn of pure gold which was used by Henry VIII, a casket in mother-of-pearl, and a very large marble incense-burner. There is also a most interesting and ingenious musical instrument made in Germany which is decorated with glass of different colours and is studded with jewels. Inside is the Queen's cipher with these verses:

> *Cantabis moneo, quisquis cantare rogaris,*
> *Vivat ut aeternos ELISABETHA dies.*

and over the keyboard:

> *Phoebe ades et modulos cum tractat pollice princeps,*
> *Fac resonent placidum tinula corda melos.*

There is also an extraordinary receptacle for combs (a kamfutter) which is shaped like a man, and a pair of gilded spurs which belonged to Henry the Eighth.

After seeing all this we carried on for another 4 miles and came to the Palace of Nonsuch, where the Court sometimes retires.

Nonsuch Palace

This is a place of such splendours that it overshadows the glory of all other buildings far and wide. That most illustrious King Henry VIII fixed upon this particularly healthy situation for it, intending it for his own pleasure and recreation, and he had it constructed with so much magnificence and splendour that you would think that he was striving for the very last word in sumptuous

259 Hentzner also quotes these lines in his description of Nonsuch, and Bentley translates:

> This, which no equal has in art or fame
> Britons deservedly do Nonsuch name.

260 'Life ends with death, glory does not die.'

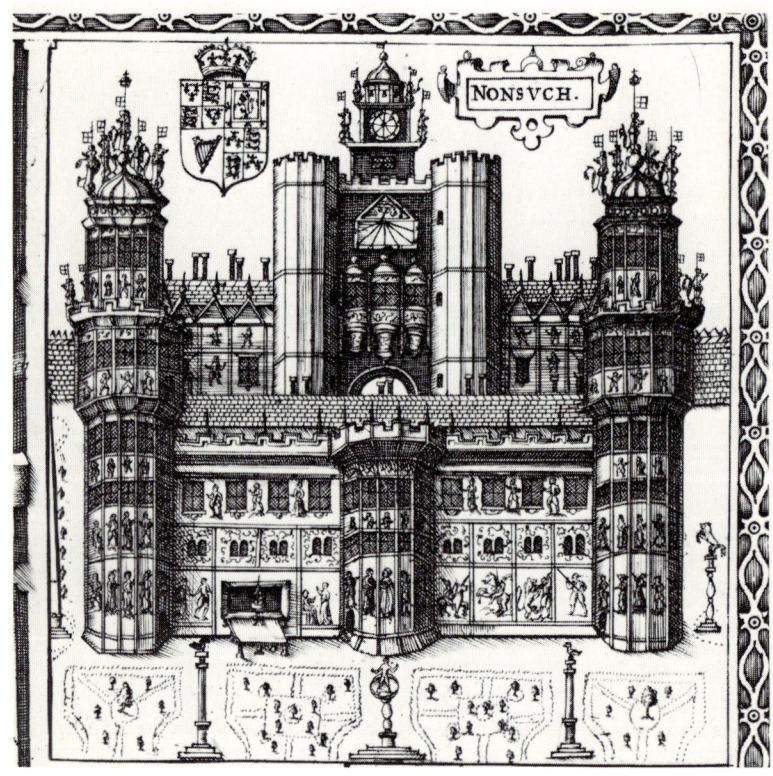

The south front of Nonsuch Palace, rising above the Privy Garden. The obelisk on a pedestal (see p. 159) is just visible at the left edge. (From John Speed's map of Surrey, 1610)

display, and at the same time cramming the sum total of all architectural skills into this one single building; and indeed, the royal possessions all about you are so inspired, there are so many miracles of perfected art and of works which rival those of ancient Rome, that with complete justification the place has been given the name, which it is in no danger of losing, which means 'Nulli Secunda' in Latin, or, as some poet puts it,

> *Hanc quia non habeat similem, laudare Britanni*
> *Soepe solent, Nullique parem cognomine dicunt,*

and indeed the parklands – well stocked with deer – which surround the palace, the choice gardens, the groves beautified with topiary work, the walks and glades shaded by the trees, all make it seem as if Loveliness herself had selected this very place to live in unity with Health.

Starting in the hall, there is a collection of sculptures representing stories from Ovid. A gilded head stands above the door with the inscription: 'Vita perit mortis, gloria non moritur.'

After mounting a few steps one sees a picture of the Roman Eagle, entirely made up of the kingdoms and provinces which came under the sway of Imperial Rome. Worth noting in one room which we entered was an extremely fine map of the world which has the eagle depicted on it; up against the wall was a 'saturnium' or basin of black marble. There were a number of portraits on the walls: Charles IX of France, Henry VIII and his wives, Elizabeth, Catherine Seymour the mother of Edward VI, who died in childbirth, and an exceedingly fine picture of Medusa with snaky locks. There is an

261 The remarkable garden was begun under Henry VIII, and completed after 1556 by Henry, Earl of Arundel, and his son-in-law John, Lord Lumley. For an account of it and further illustrations, see Martin Biddle, 'The Vanished Gardens of Nonsuch', in *Country Life*, 26 October 1961; and Roy Strong, *The Renaissance Garden in England*, London, 1979.

Pepys in 1665 clearly regretted that the glories of Nonsuch were departing, noting in his Diary on 21 September: 'and a fine place it hath heretofore been . . . I walked also in the ruined garden.'

octagonal table, a gift to the Queen, made of various sorts of different coloured stones, all fitted together with the utmost skill; the base of it is the smallest part. There is also a stonework table with 4 containers: they run with wines, beer, and water when the Queen is present. There is another map of the world which can be folded up flat, and this shows a picture of the Pyramids.

After seeing this we went down into the garden which is the finest in the whole of England, and exceedingly delightful it is. There are 3 distinct parts: the Grove, the Woodland, and the Wilderness, with a circular deerpark nearby. In the garden the Labours of Hercules and a number of other subjects from the poets are most beautifully portrayed; there are also numerous marble obelisks, including one which has been set up on a pedestal.

*Most beautifully laid out garden*

Next you go into a very spacious enclosure planted with shrubs and bushes, laid out with such distinction that whoever walks through it always longs to – and does – linger there with delight. A thing to note is the place where, upon a platform, either seated or standing, the Queen shoots at the deer: it is constructed from growing shrubs so as to make an arbour. One of the most interesting things in the garden is a walk where one can stroll completely sheltered from the sun's heat; this is because the trees are curved in shape and therefore cast a deep shadow.

From here, by going along various paths between the growing shrubs, with trees shading us from the summer heat, we entered the famous Grove of Diana, where Nature is imitated with so much skill that you would dare to swear that the original Grove of the real Diana

*Diana's Grove*

262 The inscriptions mean:

> The temptation to baseness comes not from the Goddess,
> who is chastity itself; it arises only from an evil mind
> and from an evil spirit.

> Out of an unclean spring, water defiled.
> Out of a graceless mind, a tainted view.

> Shade for the heated,
> A seat for the weary.
> Though in the shade, be not obscured
> Nor in repose acquire the serpent's view.

This summerhouse is described, and its inscriptions quoted, by Platter, who had gone round Diana's Grove in the reverse direction: 'we came to a rock out of which natural water springs into a basin, and on this was portrayed with great art and lifelike execution the story of how the three goddesses took their bath naked and sprayed Actaeon with water, causing antlers to grow upon his head, and of how his hounds afterwards tore him to pieces. Further on we came to a small vaulted temple where was a fine marble table, and the following mottoes were inscribed here thus:

On the nearest wall: 'Nil impudicum . . .'
On the right is written: 'Impuri fontis . . .'
On the left is: 'Aestuanti umbra . . .'

263 Hentzner saw this inscription, not at Nonsuch but at the entrance to Whitehall park. Probably it had been moved from there as being so much more suitable to Diana's Grove. Bentley translated it thus: 'The fisherman who has been wounded learns, though late, to beware. But the unfortunate Actaeon always presses on. The chaste virgin naturally pitied, but the powerful goddess revenged the wrong. Let Actaeon fall a prey to his dogs, an example to youth, a disgrace to those who belong to him! May Diana live, the care of Heaven; the delight of mortals; the security of those who belong to her.'

The reference to Queen Elizabeth in the final lines is clear; Horace Walpole's edition of Hentzner suggests: 'This romantic inscription probably alluded to Philip II who wooed the Queen after her sister's death; and to the destruction of the Armada.'

herself was hardly more delightful or of greater beauty. This Grove is approached by a gentle slope leading down from the garden by a path half hidden in the shade of trees. Before you approach the actual Fountain of Diana you will pass a small stone building where there is a table made from a rectangular piece of black marble. On the walls of this summerhouse you can read in golden lettering:

*Nil impudicum pudicitia Dea, nil turpe suadet, sceleris vindicta, sed mala mens, malus animus.*

also:

*Impuri fontis impuri rivuli;
Ingratae mentis impuri oculi.*

also:

*Aestuanti umbra, languenti sedes. Noli in umbra umbratilis esse, nec sint sedenti serpentis oculi.*

After seeing this summerhouse we were taken along the path which leads to the Fountain of Diana itself. This spring rises in a secluded glade at the foot of a little cliff. The source was from a number of pipes hidden in the rock, and from them a gentle flow of water bathed Diana and her two nymphs; Actaeon had approached; he was leaning against a nearby tree to hide himself and gazing lecherously at Diana; she, with a slight gesture of her hand towards him, was slowly changing his head to that of a stag; his 3 hounds were in close pursuit.

Diana's Fountain

We followed the same path to a fairly high arch which is hedged all round with a thicket of shrubs. Here on the arch was the inscription:

*Ictus piscator sapit: sed infelix Actaeon semper praeceps. Casta virgo facile miseretur: sed potens Diana scelus ulciscitur. Praeda canibus, exemplum juvenibus, suis dedecus pereat Actaeon. Cura coelitibus, chara mortalibus, suis securitas vivat Diana.*

264     Goddess, delighting most to see
       The chase, the shady clearing, and
       The running stream, the forest tree:
       Who, by the chaste power of thy hand
     Dost rule the nymphs and spirits of the land:
       How is it that the world's affairs
       Leave thee untouched by any cares,
      And why are man's embraces shunned by thee?

       From Hymen's bounteous rites, say why
       With icy beauty thou dost fly?
       Ah! it is this: 'A goddess-mind
       Consorts not well with humankind'
      So stands the fixed decree of gods on high.

265  Whatever man, like Actaeon, stands lecherously by
    Giving free rein to base desirings, both of mind and eye,
    He out of man a monster makes: he gives – a beast indeed –
      His flesh to his own dogs, which they devour.
    That man, love-mad, who sets aflame his lechery and greed
    Put the control of his own passions far beyond his power.

266 (In the first line Waldstein miscopied, writing 'victor' instead of 'pictor'.)

      You would resent the artist who portrayed
      A man's head or a dog's on the neck of a steed;
      On this neck of mine Diana a stag's head laid:
      Pity me, victim of this unjust deed.

267 Fortunately Hentzner also quotes these lines, so it is possible to correct Waldstein's numerous inaccuracies; these were probably due to the difficulty of making notes in a garden. Hentzner's version reads:

     *Mente opus humana, ne feros in corpore mores,*
      *Parrhasius pingat, Praxitilesve dolet..*
     *Cervina Actaeon tua sunt praecordia; quidni*
      *Cornua sint? prudens pectora stulta queror.*

  That is:

      Essential to the human frame
      Are human manners: otherwise
      Parrhasius must needs devise
      A brutish heart in human guise,
    Praxiteles perforce must sculpt the same.
      Actaeon, have you horns? They grew
      Revealing the stag's heart in you;
    More wise myself, such foolish hearts I blame.

  Parrhasius was a Greek painter legendary for the realism of his work.

268 Louis Frederick, son of the Duke of Württemberg, also commented upon the beauty of this garden, and Camden mentions it in *Britannia*. [*continued on p. 164*]

At the highest point of this arch there are 3 eagles; in the centre there is a stone column with a number of pipes spouting water which was spraying the bystanders. Not far from here is a small building; on the front of it is 'Diana's Grove', and the following lines:

> *O Dea qui sylvas, fontes, umbram atque venatum*
> *Expetis, et nymphas et rustica numina casto*
> *Dirigis imperio, cur te commercia Mundi*
> *Non tangunt? hominum cur non amplexibus haeres?*
> *Cur Hymaenea fugis niveo perfusa decore?*
> *Scilicet hominae divina monilia sorti*
> *Non bene conveniunt: sic stat sententia Divum.*

264

and in another place:

> *Quisquis ut Actaeon grassante libidine, nullos*
> *Imponit frenos, oculis animique furori,*
> *Bellua fit monstrumque hominum, semenque vorandum*
> *Dat canibus propriis, dum timens affectibus ignes*
> *Subiicit, et nullo retinet moderamine sensus.*

265

In the same place are these lines on Actaeon:

> *Splen copes humano capiti si victor equinas*
> *Iungere cervices, aut canis ora velit.*
> *Cervinum Diana caput cervicibus istis*
> *Addit in injustum viscera justa rogo.*

266

and on Diana:

> *Mente opus humanum referes in corpore mores*
> *Parrhasius pingat, Praxitilesve dolet,*
> *Cervina Actrontua sint praecordia quidni*
> *Cornua sint prudens pectora stulta queror.*

267

268 We made a 4 mile detour via Beddington in order to see a most lovely garden belonging to a nobleman called Francis Carew. A little river runs through the middle of this garden, so crystal-clear that you can see the water-plants beneath the surface. A thing of interest is the oval

Beddington

Sir Francis Carew was experienced in the theory as well as in the aesthetics of horticulture. Shortly after Waldstein's visit the Queen herself stayed at Beddington, and either then or during her visit in August of the previous year, Sir Francis entertained her with what Sir Hugh Platt, in *Flora's Paradise* (1608), calls 'a pretty conceit': 'Sir Francis Carew ... led her Majestie to a cherrie tree, whose fruite hee had of purpose kept backe from ripening, at the least one month after all cherries had taken their farewell of England. This secret he performed by straining a tent or cover of canvas over the whole tree, and wetting the same now and then with a scoop or horne, as the heate of the weather required: and so, by witholding the sunne beames from reflecting uppon the berries they grew both great and were very long before they had gotten their perfect cherrie-colour; and when hee was assured of her Majesties comming he removed the tent, and a few sunnie daies brought them to their full maturitie.'

269 The industry lasted almost to the end of the eighteenth century. There are several references to the trade in Elizabethan literature: Greene, in his *Quip for an Upstart Courtier* (1592), writes: 'Though I am black I am not the Devil, but indeed a collier of Croydon.'

270 The *Bear* (or *White Bear*) had just been rebuilt; she obviously gave the impression of being a completely new vessel.

271 This description suggests a straight drop from the entry port into the skiff, whereas the usual means of entry into a large ship moored to a buoy (Dr McGowan of the National Maritime Museum informed me) was by means of a rope ladder hung from the entry port, which could be either a removable section of the rail on the upper deck or an aperture in the gun deck below.

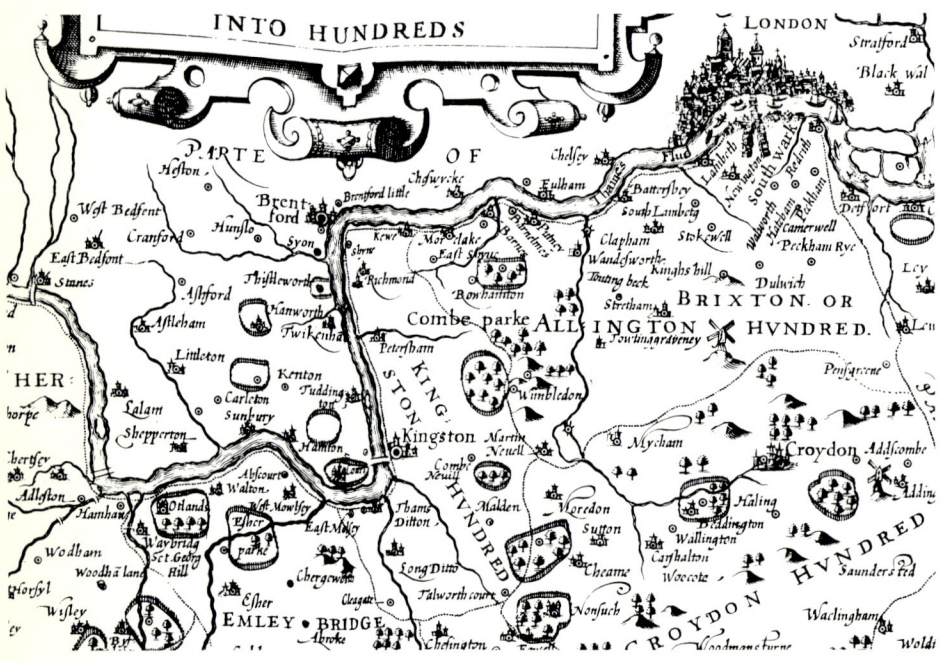

Part of Speed's map of Surrey, 1610, showing the area visited by Waldstein between 25 and 28 July. Staines is on the Thames at the far left; following the river, Hampton Court is the encircled park in the south-eastern bend, Richmond in the bend where it flows north and east again. Nonsuch is in the centre at the bottom, shown as a park, as is Beddington, to the north-east, beyond which lies Croydon.

fish-pond enclosed by trim hedges. The garden contains a beautiful square-shaped rock, sheltered on all sides and very cleverly contrived: the stream flows right through it and washes it all around. In the stream one can see a number of different representations: the best of these is Polyphome playing on his pipe, surrounded by all kinds of animals. There is also a Hydra out of whose many heads the water gushes.

After one more mile we reached the town of Croydon which lies at the foot of hilly country. It is famous for its Palace of the Archbishops of Canterbury – also for its charcoal which is a local industry. Here we made some purchases, and after 6 more miles by God's good grace we arrived safely back in London.

### Thursday, 27 July

Went out in the afternoon to see over the Queen's vessel called the *New White Bear*: this ship has only very recently been completed and is most splendidly equipped. After seeing it, as I was coming down out of the exit into the skiff which was waiting to take me off, the strength of the current forced the skiff away from the ship's side so that I all but fell into the Thames. By God's special mercy, however – He gave strength and endurance to the shoulders of Meyer who was holding me – I was saved. For the whole of the time that I was over the side Meyer held me, clutching me with his hands under my armpits until the skiff was brought back to pick me up properly. May God be praised for sparing my life in this way, and for granting me life and health that I may use them faithfully to His glory.

NB.

272 At the Steelyard, in Lower Thames Street (where Cannon Street Station now stands), a branch of the Hanseatic League had been established as early as 1266.

The German merchants were known as 'Easterlings', hence the word 'sterling', since their gold was of such high standard that it was adopted for the English currency. Grenade (1578) describes them: 'En cete mesme rue [Thames Street] est la maison des Austerlings. Ce sont marchands allemans: et font une commune despence pour le manger et le boire. Ils sont tellement reglez que c'est une chose fort honorable de voir leur ordre et maniere de faire. Ils ne leur est permis soy marier tant qu'ils seront de la dite maison, combien qu'on ne les peut contraindre au celibat: seulement s'ils se marient ils ne sont plus de la dite maison. Ils vivent et prenent leur repas en commun, et sont environ de dix et huit a vingt maistres, et autant d'autres qui sont sous eux et leurs inferieurs ...

Le nom commun de cete maison est les Stillardes, laquelle est tres magnifique et noble et riche.'

In 1597 Queen Elizabeth deprived the Easterlings of their long-enjoyed privileges in retaliation for the Emperor Rudolph's expulsion of the Merchant Venturers from Stade near Hamburg.

273 Is there a mother who could wish, though cruel and unkind,
To wipe out every memory of her own child from her heart?
Perchance it may be so; not thus, Most Gracious God, Thou art,
Thy love for us is such that we are ever in Thy mind.

274 The account of Richmond up to the end of this paragraph is taken from Camden's *Britannia*.

275 Anne was not the daughter but the sister of Wenceslaus. Her father was the Emperor Charles IV.

276 'Shene' meant resplendent or beautiful.

FRIDAY, 28 JULY

Began with a visit to the German house which is beside the Thames. The place was acquired some long time ago by German merchants who obtained it partly by purchase and partly as a reward for services rendered to the kings of England. These merchants used to enjoy a good many privileges, all of which have been taken away by the present Queen Elizabeth.

There is a picture on the wall of this house of a mother suckling her child, with the verses:

> Ecqua adeo esse potest immiti pectore mater
> Ipsa sui ut partus non meminisse velit?
> Si qua tamen talis, non tu Deus optime nostri,
> Tantus amor tuus est, non meminisse potes.

From here we took a small boat for an excursion 5 miles out of London to Richmond Palace. It was in this palace that the great warrior King Edward III died; he and his son by their successful campaigns all over France inspired so much terror that the father, like Antiochus, was called 'the Thunderbolt' and his son, like Pyrrhus, got the well-deserved nickname of 'the Eagle'. Anne, the Queen of Richard II and daughter of the Emperor Wenceslaus, also died here: it was she who first taught Englishwomen to ride on horseback as they do nowadays; before her time they used to ride in a rather unbecoming way with their legs astride like a man. The palace here used to be so splendid that it was called 'Sheen'; the royal residence was burned right down to the ground by a disastrous fire in the reign of Henry VII; then, by the efforts of that King it rose again from its ashes in great splendour just like the Phoenix, and received the new name of 'Richmond' after the place

*The royal palace of Richmond*

# RICHMOND PALACE, LONDON

*Richmond Palace. We are looking east, towards the City, where Anthonis van den Wyngaerde shows the great spire of St Paul's still piercing the horizon. (Detail. Ashmolean Museum, Oxford)*

277 The seat of Henry VII's earldom was Richmond in Yorkshire. Richmond Palace was completed in 1501; it was ruinous by the mid-seventeenth century.

278 Tides regularly reached Richmond – and even as far as Hampton Court – until the nineteenth century, when Teddington Weir and the Richmond Half-Tide Barrier were built. Now it is only in times of exceptional drought that a high spring tide may flow up to Richmond and on to Kingston. (My thanks to Mr R. D. Hughes of the Thames Conservancy for this information.)

279 The Duke of Stettin-Pomerania's Diary tells the story in greater detail: 'In the apartment next to it [i.e. next to the room in which Henry VIII died] the king's father kept a great treasure secretly hidden underneath the floor, and made his servant, to whom he confided it, swear not to reveal anything about this money to Henry VIII whose behaviour was rather wild, unless some great distress should befall the realm. As however after his father's death the son took to his studies with great diligence, the servant showed him the place, and this said treasure was spent in obtaining the costly tapestries in Hampton Court and the other royal houses.'

280 We learn from Cromwell's valuation that this bed had, very appropriately, '7 curtaines of sea water greene'. The quilts and valance were of hair-coloured (light brown) tinsel. (Millar, *Inventories*.)

281 There should have been a heading here, 'Sunday, 30 July'. The official attendance by the Lord Mayor at St Paul's for the morning service, and also Waldstein's visit to the Beargarden, show it to have been a Sunday.

282 William Ryder was Lord Mayor from November 1599 to November 1600. He was knighted in 1601.

which before he became King had been the seat of his earldom. Right up to here the tides of the open sea affect the Thames, a distance from the sea of some 50 English miles.

In the palace we were shown the room where they told us that the treasure chest of Henry VII has been concealed. The King had charged an English nobleman, the only man who knew the secret, never to reveal its existence to his son Henry VIII unless he should see him reduced to the very direst need.

The next sight is Henry VII's library: it contains all kinds of books, the majority of them in French. Note also a chess set together with an inkstand of fine workmanship, and, beautifully set out on parchment, a genealogy of the kings of England which goes back to Adam. *Library of Henry VII*

We came out of this library through an extremely long gallery, the longest we have seen anywhere in England, and then had a look at another gallery: this runs alongside the garden where there is a notable pine tree which is ingeniously propped up with artificial supports. In one of the palace rooms can be seen a bed which looks like a boat.

SATURDAY, 29 JULY
Wrote up my Diary.

We saw the Governor of the City (they call him 'My Lord Mayor') leaving St Paul's (they hold open-air services there which last for 3 hours) wearing a purple robe and a gold chain, and mounted on a horse with

*The Lord Mayor of London leaving church in procession. This drawing, made for a Dutch visitor to the City about 1614/15, shows the Mayor on his white horse, followed by Sheriffs and Aldermen and preceded by officials carrying the mace — stolen in 1627: see pp. 176–77 — and sword. (From the Autograph Album of Michael van Meer. Edinburgh University Library)*

283    The Beargarden was on the South Bank in an area known as Paris (or Parish) Garden, which lay slightly to the west of the Globe Theatre. Bearbaitings took place twice a week, on Sundays and Thursdays; Sunday seems to have been the more popular day, but after an accident when some of the stands collapsed and eight spectators were killed during a Sunday performance (an accident which many Elizabethans not unnaturally attributed to direct Divine retribution for Sabbath-breaking), Sunday bearbaiting had been prohibited for a while. This prohibition was soon allowed to lapse, and was not reintroduced until after the accession of James I, when Henslowe and Alleyn, who had a financial interest in the bearbaiting, petitioned: 'In the late quenes tyme fre libertie was permited with owt restrainte to bayght them which now is tacken a way frome vs especiallye one the Sondayes in the after noone after devine service which was the cheffest meanes and benefit to the place.' (See E. K. Chambers, *The Elizabethan Stage*, II, London, 1923, p. 471.) Bearbaiting as a spectacle is described in detail by Grenade, who shared contemporary enthusiasm for the shows at 'Parishe-gardin': 'J'ay autres fois veu lascher 14 dogues a une fois contre un Ours, et en embrassant six a la fois, les serroit si fort entres ses bras qu'il en étoufoit deux: les autres estoyent bien aises, aveques peine, d'eschaper et n'y retourner plus.'

Grenade also describes the bull-baiting which took place in the same district: 'Le plaisir du combat du Taureau est quand il peut puiser quelque Dogge (ce sont chiens fort grans) avec ses cornes, il le iette en l'aer fort haut, et cheant enterre il meurt ou se rompt quelque membre et ne vaut plus rien.'

284    Satan's dungeons are more cruel, here our prisonment is light,
Hell is endless, never-ceasing, here we have the end in sight;
Patient here through life we go lest Satan drag us down below.
From such prison shall you never be to Hell's dark region sent
Where the Stygian Lake infernal echoes cries of punishment.

saddle and bridle of gold. Before him a sword was carried, its scabbard covered in silk.

In the afternoon we went to see the bears. During the morning Monsieur Momart and Meyer, who have been our travelling companions the whole way from Canterbury to London, depart; and after dinner – and a mild celebration – the Windischgraetzes, who are going off to Belgium, also say goodbye.

Monday, 31 July

Monsieur Lesieur came to lunch with us. In the afternoon we went out and saw 6 girls – sisters, and of good family – who sang and played most beautifully on various kinds of musical instruments. The father of these girls, because he is a vigorous supporter of the Roman Catholic faith and refuses to attend Protestant services, is committed into custody (a mild custody however) and has been stripped of the greater part of his property, paying a fine in the Queen's name of 20 English pounds, i.e. $66\frac{1}{2}$ crowns, per month.

NB.

His daughters live at their father's house but are not confined to it. The following lines are written on the wall, composed, it is said, by the father:

> *Hic levis est carcer, crudelior ille Gehennae;*
> *Illius est finis, nullus at huius erit.*
> *Hic agimus nostram patienti pectore vitam,*
> *Ne simus inviti perda Gehenna tibi.*
> *Illas ex isto vitabis carcere poenas,*
> *Quas resonant Stygii tartara nigra lacus.*

## AUGUST

Tuesday, 1 August

We were invited to a very grand dinner by the Governor

285 'Long live Charles and Henry, each of them a Defender, Henry of the Faith, and Charles of the Church.'

286 Walter (later Sir Walter) Cope was a Fellow of the Society of Antiquaries and had a private museum which was visited by a number of other diarists. Platter gives a long list of the objects which he saw in Cope's collection.

287
        Like Earth's changing seasons, we
        Change as each hour slides away.
        All you see is his today,
        Mine tomorrow it will be,
        After? whose I cannot say.

or Mayor of London, and we were most courteously received. There were 13 attendants in robes who served at the table. Incidentally it is worth mentioning here that the majority of those who are chosen to be Mayors are men who are very wealthy and who are therefore able, throughout their year of office, to keep open house like princes, since the Mayor gets a mere 2,000 English pounds for his expenses, whereas he actually spends over £8,000.

*Note that the Mayor has his own swordbearer*

We then went into the Mansion House where we saw these lines:

> *Carolus Henricus vivant defensor uterque,*
> *Henricus fidei, Carolus Ecclesiae.*

## Wednesday, 2 August
Went to see an English play.

## Thursday, 3 August
Went out to see the house of a certain Monsieur Cope: it is not especially pretentious or large, but is pleasant and well-proportioned. It contains some fine pictures, and it also has a very lovely garden with a well-kept shady walk all round it. On the house these lines are written:

> *Alternante moras Mundo mutamur in horas*
> *Omnia nunc huius, mea cras, post nescio cuius.*

## Friday, 4 August
After going to see, at the house of Master Linyard the tailor, a looking-glass of great value and of equally great beauty (valuable for the jewels which sparkled all around it, beautiful for the human figures sculpted with extreme

288 The description of London Bridge is derived from Camden.

289 Waldstein's account of the Royal Exchange is taken from Camden.
The building was indeed modelled on the Bourse at Antwerp, and was built by Flemish craftsmen with materials brought from Flanders. It was completed in 1567 and ceremoniously opened by the Queen in 1571. It was destroyed in the Great FIre of 1666.
Grenade gives a detailed description of the Royal Exchange; he explains that because each country had its own section of the building it was quite easy to locate foreign merchants and get business done. It was a great place also for the delivery of letters and messages, and an important centre of news from abroad. He describes the quadrangle as being paved with small cobblestones and capable of containing (even when excluding the covered walk around it) up to 4,000 merchants. Above the gate on the south side was a high turret with a bell which was rung when business closed, i.e. at midday and at 6 p.m. The Royal Exchange also had a recreational use at weekends. From two handsome galleries below the bell turret 'les ioueurs d'instrumens de la Cité front merveilles de sonner, les dimenches a 4 heures apres midi au long iours, au grand contentement des écoutans, desquels le nombre est fort grand.'

290 London Stone appears to have been one of the minor sights of the City. Grenade describes it as deeply set into the ground half-way up Draper Street, the exposed part being about 3 feet tall, 2 feet wide and 1 foot thick (90 by 60 by 30 cm), and states that it was placed there by order of King Lud himself.
London Stone still exists, though now only a fraction of its original size; it probably suffered in the Great Fire. It stands behind a grille in the wall of a block of offices on the north side of Cannon Street, almost opposite Cannon Street Station.
The Stone is now believed to have been the *milliarium* from which distances were measured from London in Roman times.

291 Camden refers to them as 'very goodly conduits or cisterns castellated'. The best example of a conduit to survive is the one at Cambridge known as Hobson's Conduit.

The Royal Exchange. (Detail of an etching by Hollar, 1644. British Museum, London)

f.179  skill in precious stones), we set off on our journey away from London.

There are several important things about London, however, which I have not yet mentioned:

288  First of all the Bridge: this is an amazingly skilful construction of solid stonework with 19 arches; it has extremely fine buildings all along it like a street, making it easily one of the finest bridges in the whole of Europe, both for size and beauty.

1. The Bridge

Then there is the Merchants' House or Bourse (the Queen has named it 'The Royal Exchange'), which forms a quadrangle just like the one at Antwerp, and is used for commerce and banking. There is a further gallery upstairs in which all kinds of merchandise are on

2. The Bourse

289  sale. Over the entrance, and in other parts of the building also, are the royal arms surrounded by the Garter with the usual inscription, 'Honi soit qui mal y pense', and the Queen's motto, 'Dieu et mon droict', beneath.

Thirdly there are the streets, most of which are rather dark and narrow. The Goldsmiths' street is a distinguished one, very wide and with fine buildings: it gives a very rich display of gold and silver and jewels. Near it is another street called 'London Stone' because of a stone there which goes by this name; it is said to have

3. The Streets

290  stood there before London itself existed. Another thing of interest is the system by which water is brought to every part of the city by underground channels and pipes: very decorative water towers stand at the

291  distribution points. Quite recently a new aqueduct has been built to run into the city; in this the inventive skill of a German hydraulic engineer has made use of a wheel

292 This information also comes from Camden's *Britannia*.

293 Waldstein's description of the City Government was kindly read for me by Miss Betty R. Masters, Deputy Keeper of the Corporation of London Records. I am endebted to her for notes 293–296.

The Lord Mayor did not strictly represent the Queen, as he was elected annually by the citizens. His 'deputies' were the Sheriffs of London and Middlesex. The 'districts or divisions' are the wards. There were 25 City wards; a 26th was created in 1550 (the Ward of Bridge Without) when the City acquired the rights of the Crown over Southwark.

294 This refers to the annual procession to and service at St Mary Spital (originally the Priory Church of the Hospital of St Mary without Bishopsgate), which had a pulpit cross in the churchyard similar to that at St Paul's.

295 This sword is known as the Pearl Sword. The scabbard is now adorned with 2,659 pearls, but their arrangement is not original.

The 'staff' was probably the mace, made in 1559 to be carried before the Lord Mayor. It is described in 1600 as being made of silver but may well have been silver-gilt. It was stolen in 1627.

296 The Collar of SS is still worn by the Lord Mayor on ceremonial occasions. It was given to the City by Alderman Sir John Aleyn in 1545.

London Bridge, looking upstream towards Old St Paul's. The waterwheel devised by the Dutch engineer Pieter Morice in 1580 to supply the City can be seen under the arch at the far right. The artist has included an out-of-scale representation of the sort of small passenger boat that Waldstein repeatedly used. (From the Autograph Album of Michael van Meer, c. 1614/15. Edinburgh University Library)

to bring Thames water to a large part of the City through pipes which have been carefully sited in order to give the water a downward flow.

292

The City Government is organized as follows: civic authority is in the hands of a Mayor, who represents the Queen, and of his two deputies. The City is divided into 25 districts or divisions with their own Senators (they call them 'Aldermen'). Every year a new Lord Mayor is chosen, and from the moment of his election he has to hold open house to everyone and continue to do so for the whole year of his office.

London's form of government

293

On the second Feast Day of Easter they hold a celebration in his honour, in roughly the following way:

294

Before him go 40 civil servants or public officials, followed by a group bearing a sword with its scabbard encrusted with pearls, and also a golden staff like a sceptre. Two youths then follow in fine robes and wearing gold chains. After these comes My Lord Mayor himself, mounted on a white horse, with the Bishop of London at his side. The Mayor wears a crimson robe, its collar lined with black silk. Over his shoulders hangs a great chain, such as the Knights of the Garter wear. His horse is caparisoned with trappings and a bridle of black silk, all tipped with silver gilt. Two Aldermen are always in attendance on the Mayor and both wear robes of the same colour as his own; after these come secretaries and clerks on foot. The wives of these men, gorgeously dressed in red gowns and wearing gold chains, go on foot to the place, which is outside the City walls, where the service is to be held, and they return in procession to the City in the same way.

f.180

295

296

The City is said to have 120 churches, in all of which

297 This was the *Golden Hind*, originally known as the *Pelican* but renamed by Drake in compliment to Sir Christopher Hatton who had helped to promote the famous voyage. Hatton's crest was 'a hind statant or' – a standing golden hind.
   It had been intended to preserve the *Golden Hind* at Deptford for ever, in memory of Drake's magnificent achievement; this excellent idea failed, however, for souvenir hunters appear to have completed what rot had begun, and as early as 1614 Eisenberg speaks of 'Drake's ship at Deptford, nearly all destroyed'. It had been more impressive in Hentzner's time: 'Upon taking the air down the river, the first thing that struck us was the ship of that noble pirate, Sir Francis Drake, in which he is said to have surrounded this globe of earth.'

298 'Candish' was a common alternative form of 'Cavendish'.

299 Cavendish had almost completed his circumnavigation of the world when he ran into a severe storm; his ship, the *Desire*, finally made Plymouth almost without any sails at all. In the following year he sailed her round to Greenwich in order to show off to the Queen the booty he had taken from the Spaniards.
   Captain Francis Allen refers to this trip in 1589 in a letter to Anthony Bacon: 'The passing up the river of Thames by Mr Cavendish is famous, for his mariners and soldiers were clothed in silk, his sails of damask, his top-masts cloth of gold, and the richest prize that ever was brought at one time into England'. (See Birch, *Elizabeth*, I, 57.)

300 Rochester was the chief naval dockyard at the time, and the ships which Waldstein saw there comprised almost all the warships then stationed in English waters. Rathgeb and his master had also visited Rochester to see the fleet in 1592: 'the officers conducted His Highness to the shore along which were ranged not less than forty ships of war . . . in particular we noticed the large ship called the English Lion which caused immense damage to the mighty Spanish Armada a few years ago.'

301 Waldstein's ignorance of English resulted in several miscopyings from the list of ships lying at anchor in Rochester. The letter 'f' in *Swiftsure*, for instance, he mistakes for a long 's', giving the name as *'Swisthowe'*, and, never having met the word 'gilliflower', he transcribes it *'Jeheflower'*. I have to thank the National Maritime Museum at Greenwich for the correct names and also for information about these ships and the Rochester dockyard.
   Sixteen of the vessels which Waldstein saw had been in action against the Spanish Armada. They were: *Advice, Ark Royal, Antelope, Charles, Dreadnought, Elisabeth Jonas, Golden Lion, Mary Rose, Moon, Merlin, Nonpareil, Rainbow, Swiftsure, Spy, Vanguard* and *Victory*. The *Ark Royal* had been Lord Howard of Effingham's flagship.

they hold services: there are even churches where they have services in French, Italian, and Flemish.

297  Between London and Greenwich you can see Drake's ship, in which he sailed the whole way round the world.
298  Until recently there was another ship which belonged to a nobleman named Thomas Candish, and in her, in rivalry of Drake, he also circumnavigated the globe. This ship is said to have brought back an incredible amount of treasure, so that when she sailed into port at Greenwich, where the Queen then was, all her sails were made of silk and so were the ropes which stayed the mast
299  and held the anchor.

We left London together with Baron von Sonnenburg (i.e. the Margrave of Brandenburg who was travelling incognito) and Monsieur Lesieur, and reached Gravesend by boat at about mid‑day; there we dined, hired horses, and did the 5 miles to Rochester.

### Saturday, 5 August

300  In the morning we saw the Queen's ships at Rochester, 35 in number, named as follows:
I *Triumph*, II *Elisabeth Jonas*, III *Bear*, IV *Honour*, V *Ark Royal*, VI *Victory*, VII *Gardeland*, VIII *Repulse*, IX *Warspite*, X *Vanguard*, XI *Rainbow*, XII *Defiance*, XIII *Mary Rose*, XIV *Golden Lyon*, XV *Bonaventure*, XVI *Nonpareil*, XVII
f.181  *Hope*, XVIII *Dreadnought*, XIX *Swiftsure*, XX *Antelope*, XXI *Adventure*, XXII *Crane*, XXIII *Quittance*, XXIV *Answer*, XXV *Advantage*, XXVI *Tramontana*, XXVII *Charles*, XXVIII *Moon*, XXIX *Spy*, XXX *Advice*, XXXI *Merlin*, XXXII *Prime*
301  *Rose*, XXXIII *Gilliflower*, XXXIV *Mercury*, XXXV *Bonavolia*.

We went on board the two largest, the *Elisabeth* and the *Triumph*. The *Elisabeth* is an extremely handsome

302 The Queen herself had launched the *Elisabeth Jonas* at Woolwich in 1559. She is believed to have chosen this unusual name for the ship in order to commemorate her own escape from her enemies, as remarkable a deliverance, so she considered, as that of Jonah from the belly of the whale.

Although almost the oldest ship which Waldstein saw, the *Elisabeth Jonas* had been extensively rebuilt in 1597–98, and was the most splendid vessel in the whole fleet; the large sum of £180 was spent in 1598 'upon painting and gilding the ship, including the gilding of Her Majesty's whole arms and supporters on the beak head'.

303
Elizabeth! May His own power
Who is Judah's Lion divine
Glorious Flower of Jesse's line
Guard thy glories too, each hour.

So, this English race may be
Long well-pleasing to thy Grace:
They, for many a season's space
Shall rejoice in having thee:

Much to righteous men endeared,
Much too, by the wicked feared.

*A contemporary woodcut of the 'Ark Royal', flagship of the English fleet against the Armada. (British Museum, London)*

ship: she has very impressive staterooms and bears an effigy of the Queen herself. She is equipped with 67 huge cannon; in 1588 she was attacked by 14 guns of the Spanish fleet but came off undamaged.

In one of her staterooms you can see this inscription:

> *Qui Leo de Juda est, et flos de Jesse lionis*
> *Protegat et flores ELISABETHA tuos.*
> *Ut te Angli longum, longum Anglis ipsa fruaris,*
> *Tam dilecta bonis quam metuenda malis.*
> *Vivat REGINA semper eadem.*

Especially interesting here is her lantern or stern light which is made of copper and is exceptionally large. This ship is extremely lofty and has a quite enormous mast.

We passed the place where masts are put into the water without their suffering from rot, and then went over to the warehouse where ropes, sails, and other naval supplies are stored.

At about mid-day, after having hired the horses, we left Rochester for Sittingbourne which is some 10 miles off; then to Canterbury, 13 miles from Sittingbourne, and from there another 12 miles on to Dover.

## Sunday, 6 August

As we were offered a passage in a ship which was leaving without delay for Boulogne, we set sail from Dover at around noon, after having had to pay 22 English shillings each for a permit to leave the country. And thus we said goodbye to England, and with a small gale of wind – blowing on our quarter however – we were driven across to the opposite coast and in 5 or 6 hours arrived safely at Boulogne. *I was seasick.*

# NOTA BENE

I am indebted to Mr J. N. H. Lawrance, Fellow of Magdalen College, Oxford, and to Miss E. M. Furze, M.A., of St Hilda's College, Oxford, for having 'vetted' my translation of Waldstein's Diary. They have a far greater knowledge of the niceties of classical and Renaissance Latin than I, and had no difficulty in pointing out numerous minor (and two or three major) errors which I had made. I can admit to these mistakes quite cheerfully in view of the fact that even the great classical scholars have occasionally nodded. Benjamin Jowett himself, when Master of Balliol, asked the poet Swinburne to check his *Plato's Dialogues* against the original Greek before the proofs went back to the printers. E. F. Benson records that some undergraduates attending a tutorial in the Master's rooms one morning were enduring Jowett's withering sarcasms upon their stupidity when they heard a crow of delight from the adjoining study, followed by Swinburne's voice joyfully uplifted: 'Another howler, Master!' There was a little silence. Then: 'Thank you, Algernon' said Jowett – and closed the door.

# INDEX

Page numbers in *italic* indicate illustrations.
Portraits are indexed by name. Other works of art are indexed under 'pictures' and 'sculptures'.

ALABASTER, William 103
Althorp 114–15
Ammianus Marcellinus 35
Anne of Bohemia 167
Anthony of Francktrue (?) 57
Antwerp 153, 175
BEAUMONT, Robert 103
Beddington 163–65, *164*
Bibliander (Buchmann), Theodor 52, 55
Bibye, Simon 88
bird of paradise 141
Black Prince (Edward, Prince of Wales) 29–31, 167
Bodley, Sir Thomas 131
Boleyn, Anne 139, 145
Boulogne 43, 45, 149, 181
Brackley 117
Brandenburg, Margrave of 24, 179
Bruchelle, William 31
Bullinger, Heinrich 52, 55, 61
Burghley House 111–13, *110*
Burgundy, Charles, Duke of 45
CADIZ 105, 107
Cadwallader, King 63
Caesar, Julius 45, 71, 147, 149
Caesars 85, 87, 147
Caius, John 63, 88, 92
Calais 12, 25
Cambridge 61, 63, 87–109, *86*, *92*; Commencement 93–95, 97–101; dates and founders of colleges 91–93; Castle 105; Christ's College 91, 105, *108*; Emmanuel College 91, 105, *pl. IV*; King's College 89, 105–7, 139; Magdalene College 91, 103–5; Peterhouse College 89, 95–97, 99, 101; St Catharine's College 91, 98; St John's College 91, 103; Sidney Sussex College 91, 105, *90*; Trinity College 60, 91, 101–3
Camden, William 162; as source for the diarist 32–35, 36–37, 40–41, 62, 89, 110–11, 114–15, 116–17, 118–19, 120–21, 137–39, 142–43, 154–57, 166–67, 174–75
Canterbury 29–33, 171, 181
Canterbury, Archbishops of 28, 59, 61, 165, *60*
Carew, Sir Francis 163, 164
Case, John 129
Catherine of Aragon 51
Cavendish (Candish), Sir Thomas 179
Cecil, Sir Robert 24, 59, 60, 71–73, 80, 81, 116, *82*
Cecil, William 81, 111
Cecil family portraits 85
Charles V, Emperor 45, 47, 57, 143, 153
Charles IX of France 157
Chatillon, Cardinal 31
Cicero, *De Officiis* 105, *pl. IV*
Coligny, Gaspard de, Comte (Admiral of France) 85
Collyweston 113
Condé, Louis, Prince de 85
Cope, Walter 173
Coryat, Thomas 18–19, 52, 58
Croydon 165, *164*
DAVID II of Scotland 139, 141
Desmond, James Fitzgerald, 'Queen's Earl' of 71
Dover 25–29, 181
Drake, Sir Francis 179
Dunkirk 27
Duns Scotus 135
EDWARD I of England 41
Edward III of England 61, 101, 139, 143, 167
Edward IV of England 85, 143, 145
Edward VI of England 139, 141, 149, 153; depictions of 43–45, 47, 61, 85–87, 153, *pl. II*, *44*
Egmont, Count 85
Eisenberg, Peter 18, 50, 118, 152
Elizabeth I, Queen of England: imprisoned 71, 117; orders a check on foreign visitors 27; receives the diarist 73–81; dining ceremony 81; decides in favour of Trinity College, Cambridge 103; withdraws privileges from German merchants 167; fines Catholics 171
– depictions of 45, 47, 61, 85, 151, 157, *pl. III*, *48*, *76*, *142*; furnishings and rooms associated with 49–51, 141, 151, 153, 155, 159; inscriptions alluding to 45, 47, 59, 107, 115, 147, 149,

182

155, 161, 181; writings by 51,
  117–19
– and the *Elisabeth Jonas* 180,
  181; at Greenwich 73–81, 179;
  at Nonsuch 159; at Theobalds
  83, at Whitehall 43, 49–51,
  57; at Windsor 139, 141
Elizabeth of York 41, 57
Elizabeth, Queen of Spain 47
Elizabeth, Queen of
  Transylvania 45
Ely Cathedral 105
Erasmus 51
Essex, Robert Devereux, Earl of
  53, 93, 104–7
Eton College 139
FANE, Sir Thomas, Lieutenant
  ('Governor') of Dover
  Castle 25, 27–29
Fotheringhay Castle 109–11
Frederick II of Denmark 143
gardens: Beddington 163–65;
  Burghley 111; Hampton
  Court 147; London (Walter
  Cope's) 173, (Lambeth
  Palace) 63, (Whitehall
  Palace) 43, 59, *pl. I*;
  Nonsuch 157, 159–63, *156*;
  Theobalds 83, 87;
  Towcester 117
Garter, Knights of the 73, 113,
  141, 143, 177, *142*
genealogies 45, 61, 169
Gentilis, Alberic 131
Gerschow, Frederick (diarist for
  Duke of Stettin-Pomerania)
  18
globes 45, 85
Gloucester, Humphrey, Duke of
  125, 130
Godmanchester 109
Godstow 121
Gravesend 33, 179
Greenwich 73–81, 179, *72*
Grenade, L. 18, 34, 36, 62, 166,
  170, 174
Grynaeus (Gryner), Simon 55
Gualter (Qwalter), Rudolf 52,
  55
HALES, Sir James 29
Hampton Court Palace 42,
  145–55, *144*, *148*, *164*
Hatton, Sir Christopher 65,
  113, 115
Helmstadt (or Helmstedt) 57
Henry I of England 117
Henry II of England 119
Henry IV of England 31, 85
Henry V of England 85, 141
Henry VI of England 85, 115
Henry VII of England 41, 57,
  72, 85, 167–68, *40*
Henry VIII of England:
  depictions of 43, 45, 57, 151,
  157, *48*, *150*; inscriptions
  alluding to 47, 57, 61, 63,
  173; objects and furnishings
  associated with 51, 139, 145,
  149, 151, 155, 169, *68–69*
– and Greenwich 72; and
  Nonsuch 155; and
  Whitehall 42
Henry III of France 143, *142*
Henry IV of France 143
Hentzner, Paul 17, 26, 36, 58,
  62, 64, 66, 74, 88, 104, 118,
  120, 140, 156, 160, 162, 178
Holdenby House 113–15
Holbein, Hans: *Edward VI as a
  Child* 47, *pl. II*; Whitehall
  mural 57
Holland, Lady Margaret 29
Holland, Dr Thomas 135
Huntingdon 109
ISLIP, Simon, Archbishop of
  Canterbury 31, 123
JOHN II OF FRANCE 31, 139,
  141
John of Austria, Don 85
Julius II, Pope 45
KETTERING 113
LANCASTER, Earl (error for
  Duke) of (John of Gaunt) 65
Langton, Stephen, Archbishop
  of Canterbury 33
Leicester, Earl of 115
Leinvert (tailor): *see* Linyard
Lescinsky (friend of diarist) 33
Lesieur, Stephen 73, 81, 171,
  179
Linacre, Thomas 63
Linyard the tailor (diarist's
  guide) 127, 173
London *32*; diarist in 33–73,
  81, 165–79; description of
  33–35; churches 177–79;
  government 177; streets 175;
  theatres 36, 37, *38*, 173; water
  supply 175–77
– Beargarden 171; Bridge
  37, 175, *38*, *176*; Fleur-de-Lys
  inn 33; Lambeth Palace
  59–63, *39*, *60*; London Stone
  175; Mansion House 173;
  Royal Exchange 175, *174*; St
  James's Palace and Park 43,
  59, *39*; St Paul's Cathedral
  37, 63–65, 141, 169, *168*, *176*;
  Steelyard ('the German
  House') 167; Tower of
  London 35–37, 65–71, 85,
  *68–69*; Westminster 37–43,
  59, *38*, *39*, *40*, *60*; Whitehall
  Palace 43–59, *pl. I*, *39*, *150*
London, Lord Mayor of 65,
  169–71, 173, 177, *170*
Louis XII of France 42, 45
Lovelace, William 29
MAIDS OF HONOUR 73
de Maisse (Ambassador) 42
Mandelslo, Albert de 84, 86
Manningham, John 52
maps 45, 45, 61, 157, 159
Mary, St (the Virgin Mary) 45,
  63, 85, 143
Mary I, Queen of England 51,
  63, 85, 117
Mary, Queen of Hungary 47
Mary, Queen of Scots 109–11,
  153
Maximilian I, Emperor 43, 45,
  143, *48*
Maximilian, Archduke 27
Meyer (diarist's travelling
  companion) 165, 171
Momart (diarist's travelling
  companion) 171
Mompelgard, Count 18; *and see*
  Württemberg, Frederick of
Morice, Pieter (engineer)
  175–77, *176*
Morley, Christopher 101–3
Mountjoy, Earl of 45
Musculus (Müslin), Wolfgang
  53
music and musical instruments
  45, 151, 155
NEVILLE, Sir Henry 73
Nonsuch Palace 155–63, *156*,
  *164*
Norfolk, Thomas Howard, 4th
  Duke of 111
Northampton 115
Northumberland, Henry Percy,
  8th Earl of 71
OECOLAMPADIUS (Hüsgen),
  Johann 55
d'Oilly, Robert 121
Orange, William, Prince of 47,
  61
Orleans 12, 27
Overall, Dr John 94, 98–99
Oxford 61, 63, 121–37, *120*,
  *132*; dates and founders of
  colleges 123–25; All Souls'
  College 123, 135; Bodleian
  Library 131, *133*; Brasenose
  College 125, 131; Christ
  Church College 123, 125,
  127–29, 137; Divinity School
  125, 131, *124*; Lincoln
  College 131; Magdalen
  College 123, 124, 129–31,

137; Merton College 123, 135; the Queen's College 123, 135, *133*; St John's (St Bernard's) College 123, 125, 129; St Mary the Virgin 126–27; Trinity (Durham) College 123, 125, 135
DE PAILLY (representative of United Provinces) 25
Parma, Alexander, Duke of 85
Pellicanus (Kürschner), Conrad 55
Philip II of Spain 143, *142*
pictures mentioned by the diarist (other than identified portraits):
 Admiral of France 85
 Antwerp 153
 'battle between Charles V and the Protestants' 57
 battle, naval, fought by Henry V 141
 battle, 'Papal' (Pavia?) 42, 45
 'battle against the Saracens in Piedmont' 45
 battle of Ravenna 45
 Brazilians 83
 the Caesars 85, 147
 Cassandra and Hector 113
 chamaeleon 63
 Christ 45, 61, 63, 149
 cities, views of 85
 cripple carried on blind man's shoulders 43
 Crucifixion, with two monks 149
 Eagle, Roman 157
 'episodes from history' 87
 fruit 47
 Greek woman 57
 Hector and Cassandra 113
 'Juno, Pallas Athene, and Venus, together with Queen Elizabeth' 47, *48*
 king sitting in judgment 153
 Knights-Commander of the Golden Fleece 85
 Last Supper 149
 'Love, represented as a virgin' 153
 Malta, Siege of 45
 Medea and Jason 111–13
 Medusa 157
 'meeting of the Emperor Maximilian I and Henry VIII near Tournai and Therouanne' 43, *48*
 mother suckling a child 167
 Obedience 153
 Revelation 31
 Scaevola before Porsena 46
Spanish Inquisition in Belgium 61
 Tarquin and Lucretia 153
 'a woman, a goldsmith's wife, said to have been Henry VIII's mistress' 45
Platter, Thomas 17, 18, 32, 36, 140, 146, 148, 150, 154, 160
Playfair (Playfere, Playford), Dr Thomas, Moderator 98–99
Pope, Sir Thomas 125, 135
Price, Hugh 125
RAINOLDS (Reynolds), John 129
Rathgeb, Jacob (diarist of Duke of Württemberg) 18, 72, 80, 82, 146
Richard I of England 121, 143
Richard II of England 42, 45
Richard III of England 85
Richmond Place 167–69, *164, 168*
Rochester 33, 179–81
Rosamund, Fair 119–21
Rowlands, Samuel 58
SAVOY, Duke of, and family 47
Saxe-Weimar, Johann Ernest, Duke of 18, 50
Saxony, Duke of 85
sculptures mentioned by the diarist (other than identified portraits):
 Actaeon 161
 animals, heraldic 59, *pl. 1*
 'Apollo and nine Muses and Athena and Mercury' 115
 Attila 43
 Caesars 85, 87, 147
 centaur 83
 Christ 83, 153
 'Diana and two nymphs, with Actaeon' 161
 gilded head 157
 Hercules, Labours of 159
 Jupiter on an eagle and the Liberal Arts 115
 Marcus Curtius 153
 Polyphome surrounded by animals 165
 'stories from Ovid' 157
Seymour, Catherine (error for Jane) 157
Sherburn (hostel-keeper at Oxford) 131
ships 165, 179–81, *180*
Sittingbourne 33, 181
Sledd, John 100
Soame, Robert, Vice-Chancellor of Cambridge University 95, 98, 99, 101, 105, 109, 127
Sonnenburg, Baron (Margrave of Brandenburg) 24, 181
Spencer, Sir John 115
Stadler (acquaintance of the diarist) 71
Staines 145, *164*
Stamford 111
Stanton, Hervey de 61
Stettin-Pomerania, Duke of 18, 70, 126, 168
Strasbourg 10–11, 12
sundials 45, 47, 83, 127
TACITUS 35
tapestries: at Hampton Court 147, 149, 151, *148*; at Theobalds 85; at Tower of London 71; at Whitehall 45, 51; at Windsor 139–41
Theobalds 81–87
Thomas Aquinas, St 31
Thomas a Becket, St 31
Thornton, Thomas, Vice-Chancellor of Oxford University 125–27, 129
Thott, Thage 18, 146
Towcester 117
ULRIK, Prince of Denmark 25
VAN DEN BRICSEN, Cornelis 20, 25
Vermigli, Pietro Martire (Peter Martyr) 52, 55, 61
WARE 87
Warwick, Richard Neville, Earl of 115
Wedel, Leopold von 18, 44
Wenceslaus, Emperor 167
Whitaker, William 103
Whitgift, John, Archbishop of Canterbury 28, 59
Whyte (White), Rowland 26, 72
Windischgraetz (brothers, friends of the diarist) 71, 135, 137, 171
Windsor Castle 137–45, *48, 136, 142*
Wolfius 105
Wolsey, Thomas, Cardinal 42, 125, 128, 145
Woodstock 117, *116*
Württemberg, Frederick, Duke of 18, 80; for his diary *see also* Rathgeb
Württemberg, Louis Frederick of 18, 162
Wycliffe, John 135
Wycombe 137
ZEUXIS 125
Zinzerling, Justus 18, 32, 42, 146, 150
Zwingli (Zvinglius), Ulrich 55, 61

184

ejus quæstionem determinabis in aurē
magistro sedendo. EXEITO.
Toto actu finito Vicecancellarium
ad collegium D. Petri prosecuti sumus, ubi convivium cui fœminæ
etiam intererant apparatum fuit.
Solent autem in ijs collegijs convivia celebrari, in quibus unus ex
promotis moratur, unde in tanta
multitudine candidatorum prope
singula collegia convivia singula
peragebant. Hic magnificè (ut
Angli peregrinos solent) excepti, et
perhumaniter tractati, domum
nos recepimus.

Die ℣. 12. Julij.

Hunc diem videndis Collegijs im-
pendimus. Primum ingressi
sumus Collegium Trinitatis, q̄
omnium est amplissimum. In eo
domus est adhuc Eduardi tertij,
qui per integram hyemem hic habita-
uit cum coniuge. In sacello ubi pre-
ces et conciones habentur, hoc legitur
Epitaphium: Christophoro Worth huius
collegij quondam socio posuit Joannes
Gleda, ibidem quondam socius.

*(margin: Collegium Trinitatis.)*